GREAT

DISCOVER THE GREAT PLAINS

Series Editor: Richard Edwards, Center for Great Plains Studies (emeritus)

JAY H. BUCKLEY &
JEFFERY D. NOKES

PLAINS

Forts

UNIVERSITY OF NEBRASKA PRESS *Lincoln*

The University of Nebraska Press is
part of a land-grant institution with
campuses and programs on the past,
present, and future homelands of
the Pawnee, Ponca, Otoe-Missouria,
Omaha, Dakota, Lakota, Kaw,
Cheyenne, and Arapaho Peoples, as well
as those of the relocated Ho-Chunk,
Sac and Fox, and Iowa Peoples.

Library of Congress
Cataloging-in-Publication Data

Names: Buckley, Jay H, author.
Nokes, Jeffery D, author.
Title: Great Plains forts / Jay H.
Buckley and Jeffery D. Nokes.
Description: Lincoln: University
of Nebraska Press, [2023] | Series:
Discover the Great Plains | "A Project
of the Center for Great Plains Studies,
University of Nebraska." | Includes
bibliographical references and index. |
Summary: "Great Plains Forts introduces
readers to the fortifications that have
impacted the lives of Indigenous peoples,
fur trappers and traders, travelers, and
military personnel on the Great Plains
and prairies from precontact times to
the present. Using stories to introduce
patterns in fortification construction and
use, Jay H. Buckley and Jeffery D. Nokes
explore the eras of fort-building on the
Great Plains from Canada to Texas.
Stories about fortifications and fortified
cities built by Indigenous peoples reveal
the lesser-known history of precontact
violence on the plains. Great Plains Forts
includes stories of Spanish presidios
and French and British outposts in their
respective borderlands. Forts played
crucial roles in the international fur
trade and served as emporiums along
the overland trails and along riverway
corridors as Euro-Americans traveled
into the West. Soldiers and families
resided in these military outposts,
and this military presence in turn
affected Indigenous Plains peoples.
The appendix includes a reference
guide organized by state and province,
enabling readers to search easily for
specific forts."— Provided by publisher.
Identifiers: LCCN 2023013537
ISBN 9781496207715 (paperback)
ISBN 9781496238207 (epub)
ISBN 9781496238214 (pdf)
Subjects: LCSH: Fortification—Great
Plains—History. | Trading posts—Great
Plains—History. | Indians of North
America—Great Plains—History. |
BISAC: HISTORY / Canada /
Provincial, Territorial & Local / Prairie
Provinces (AB, MB, SK) | HISTORY /
United States / State & Local /
Southwest (AZ, NM, OK, TX)
Classification: LCC E46.5 B83 2023 |
DDC 623.197—dc23/eng/20230613
LC record available at https://
lccn.loc.gov/2023013537

Set and designed in Garamond
Premier by N. Putens.

Dedicated to our beloved wives, Becky Buckley and Gina Nokes, for joining us on this journey.

Also dedicated to Jay's academic mentors while he earned his PhD at the University of Nebraska and was employed by the Center for Great Plains Studies: Gary E. Moulton, David J. Wishart, and John R. Wunder.

CONTENTS

ILLUSTRATIONS

ACKNOWLEDGMENTS

We are indebted to Bridget Barry, editor in chief at the University of Nebraska Press, for her sound advice and unwavering support of this project. Our sincerest gratitude goes to Richard Edwards, former director of the Center for Great Plains Studies and series editor for Discover the Great Plains. Rick's patience, encouragement, and perseverance helped us continue this project despite the limitations and delays caused by the COVID-19 pandemic. We extend our thanks to Bison Books executive editor W. Clark Whitehorn and the publication team at the University of Nebraska Press, including copyeditor Joyce Bond, design and production manager Ann Baker, and our indexer, Douglas Easton.

Jay completed his PhD in history at the University of Nebraska–Lincoln and worked as a graduate assistant at the Center for Great Plains Studies for directors John R. Wunder and James Stubbendieck. We appreciate them and their staff, as well as the center's support of Great Plains histories. We are grateful for friends and scholars who inspired and mentored us about the Great Plains, including Gary E. Moulton, David J. Wishart, John R. Wunder, and W. Raymond Wood. Friends Darian Kath, Thomas Thiessen, and Philippa Newfield made helpful suggestions on early drafts.

Our gratitude also goes to the students, faculty, and administrators at Brigham Young University who aided our scholarly efforts. Undergraduate research assistants Rachel Hogan, Stephanie King, and Andrew Cheney conducted excellent research for the chapter on Canadian Prairies posts and other chapters. History Department chair Brian Q. Cannon and college dean Laura Padilla-Walker have been especially helpful and supportive to both of us.

Most of all, we thank Becky Buckley and Gina Nokes for accompanying us on this journey of discovery of the Great Plains.

Fig. 1. The Great Plains. Courtesy Center for Great Plains Studies.

In the fall of 1845 Susan Shelby envisioned experiencing the American West firsthand, perhaps while listening to the fanciful tales told by her fiancé, Samuel Magoffin, a pioneer of the Santa Fe Trail. Eighteen-year-old Susan married Samuel, twenty-seven years her senior, that November. After their honeymoon in New York, they outfitted a merchant caravan and embarked from Franklin, Missouri, in the spring of 1846, bound for Santa Fe. Accompanied by her servant Jane and her dog Ring, Susan described herself in her journal as a wandering princess of the prairie. By July, however, she longed for the comforts she had left behind in Kentucky. Bent's Fort represented one of the few places along the Santa Fe Trail that could provide a semblance of those comforts.

Built along the Arkansas River in 1833 by Charles and William Bent and Ceran St. Vrain, Bent's Fort had become a hub of trading activity with the Cheyenne and Arapaho Nations and other fur traders operating in the region. It represented an important landmark in eastern Colorado on the Great Plains' western fringe. Bent's Fort offered travelers a place to rest, replenish supplies, make needed repairs, enjoy a game of billiards, and even drink a glass of ice water on a hot summer day. In 1846, as the Magoffins' caravan approached, excitement emanated from the soldiers assembling outside the fort in anticipation of the impending war with Mexico. After several long months on the trail, exposed to mosquitoes, predators, and thunderstorms, Susan eagerly anticipated the comforts Bent's Fort offered.

She also anticipated with nervous excitement the birth of her first child. But as the caravan approached Bent's Fort, Susan sensed something was wrong with her unborn baby. Earlier in the expedition, she had fallen from her carriage on a rough stretch of the trail. Since then, she had suffered physically and psychologically. Her detailed journal remains somewhat cryptic in her description of her symptoms—proper Victorian women did not speak openly about pregnancy. A careful reader, however, can infer that her "sickness" was pregnancy related. While resting at Bent's Fort, and under the care of the army surgeon, Susan Magoffin delivered her stillborn infant. She was devastated. Compounding her anguish, an Indigenous woman arrived at the fort and gave birth to a healthy baby the same day. Susan did not have long to mourn, however, for her caravan soon left Bent's Fort and continued toward Santa Fe.

The familiar story of the North American Great Plains is one of powerful Indigenous nations, vast bison herds, extensive prairie dog villages, and an ocean of grass waving in the wind. The narrative includes tales of Native inhabitants who met Spanish, French, and American newcomers and recounts how explorers, trappers, traders, soldiers, and settlers journeyed on Native thoroughfares and game trails along meandering rivers toward the Rocky Mountains and the sunset. Central to the story, though often forgotten, are the forts that enabled interlopers to displace and dispossess Native peoples and establish an American presence. Forts feature prominently in the journals of literate travelers like Susan Magoffin. The forts dotting the Great Plains and Canadian Prairies were influential in the lives of those whose ancestors had lived there for centuries; for those passing through on foot, on horseback, in wagons, or by railroad; and for new arrivals who hoped to call the plains home.

Forts are central to the story of the Great Plains for several reasons. They were tightly connected to the unique geography of the region. The location of Bent's Fort, for example, was strategically chosen by the Bent brothers and their business colleague, Ceran St. Vrain. Just a decade before its construction,

Fig. 2. Susan Shelby Magoffin. Wikimedia Commons.

William Becknell and other entrepreneurs blazed a route linking the Mexican settlements of Santa Fe and Taos with those of western Missouri. Susan Magoffin's husband, Samuel, amassed his fortune engaging in this Santa Fe trade. The mountain route of the Santa Fe Trail ascended the Arkansas River into eastern Colorado. Bent's Fort was positioned where the trail left the main branch of the Arkansas and roughly followed one of its tributaries, Timpas Creek, in a southwesterly direction. Its location on the edge of the plains gave travelers one last chance to enjoy the plentiful water and grass of the Arkansas River valley, rest their livestock, and prepare for the difficult mountainous route that lay ahead.

Other American forts that dotted the Great Plains were similarly constructed at key geographic locations, and many were relocated after some trial and error. Often Indigenous peoples participated in selecting suitable sites for trading posts. Sometimes they also forced posts to close or destroyed them. In 1839 African American trapper and explorer James Beckwourth, who also became a respected Crow war chief, relocated Fort Cass after the Blackfeet destroyed the first post bearing that name. Years later, as Beckwourth dictated his memoir, he remembered the process of choosing the setting for the new fort built on the high western Montana plains: "I consulted with our chiefs and braves upon the selection of a more secure location for a new fort, and it was unanimously agreed upon that the mouth of the Rose Bud [Creek], thirty miles lower down the [Yellowstone] river, offered the best situation, as the country was fair and open all round, and afforded the hostile Indians no good places of concealment. There was also a fine grazing country there, and plenty of buffalo, so that a village of the Crows could winter under the fort and afford them the protection of their presence."

BECKWOURTH.

Fig. 3. James P. Beckwourth. Wikimedia Commons.

Beckwourth's account shows that the location of forts was based not solely on the physical geography of the plains but also on human geography and interaction. Tribes of the Blackfeet Confederacy, including the Niitsitapi (Blackfoot [Siksika], Blood [Kainais], Piegan Blackfeet [Piikani], and Gros Ventres of the Prairies [Atsinas]), were intent on ending American trade with their rivals, the Shoshones (Newe) and Crows (Apsáalooke/Absarokas), forcing the abandonment of the original Fort Cass and causing its relocation. Crow leaders advised Beckwourth on prime locations for the new fort. This case was not unusual, as numerous human and environmental factors influenced fort locations. Over 500 miles to the south, Bent's Fort was built along the Arkansas River near the homes of Cheyenne and Arapaho hunters who delivered buffalo robes and other furs to the fort in exchange for guns, traps, and other goods. The purposes of the powerful nations of the Great Plains and the objectives of Native, Spanish, French, British, American, Canadian, and Mexican peoples all factored into decisions about fort locations.

Recognizing the role of forts is necessary to understand not only the stories of individuals like Magoffin and Beckwourth but also the stories of nations—Indian nations trying to preserve Indigenous sovereignty and European and American states endeavoring to establish a physical presence on the Great Plains to promote their own sovereignty over the region. For instance, Fort Cass both strengthened the American presence on the Great Plains and empowered the Crow Nation by giving it greater access to the resources already possessed by rival nations such as the Blackfeet. Beckwourth knew that the presence of Native allies strengthened Fort Cass's defenses and increased its chances of survival.

Moreover, forts play a central role in the historical record of the Great Plains because they symbolize the borderlands and contested spaces where diverse peoples met and interacted. Forts became cultural crossroads, attracting Native, Spanish, French, British, Canadian, Mexican, and American investors, traders, patrons, tourists, and adventurers. Magoffin's observation of the Indian woman who came to Bent's Fort to deliver her baby illustrates the acceptance, tolerance, and contributions of individuals from many cultures at these frontier crossroads. Beckwourth suggested that the presence of Native allies strengthened Fort Cass's defenses and helped ensure its survival. Forts represented locations where trade occurred, cross-cultural relationships formed, and treaties were negotiated and signed. Some forts became detested representations of foreign interlopers and the sites of violent battles defending Native sovereignty. Following is an overview of the fortifications constructed by the Native inhabitants of the Great Plains, as well as Spanish and Mexican, French, British, and U.S. fortifications, themes discussed in greater detail in the subsequent chapters.

Indigenous Fortifications

Warfare was common among Indigenous peoples of the Great Plains before the arrival of Europeans. Enemy nations engaged in raiding and feuds, with battles that generally involved small numbers of combatants and ritualized encounters, although they sometimes could involve armies numbering in the thousands. Archaeological evidence suggests that by 1300 AD the Mandan people who lived near the Missouri River responded to the threat their enemies posed by building defensive perimeters around their villages. Fortifications that included dry moats, timber palisades, and bastions for observation enclosed entire villages. Tribesmen located their villages at sites with natural defenses such as elevated riverbanks, bluffs, and points of land. Defensive works were present even in sites used for short durations, suggesting the high priority placed on fortifications.

One of the most important (and heavily studied) locations of Caddoan-speaking ancestral Arikara occupation within the Missouri River drainage is the Crow Creek site near modern Chamberlain, South Dakota. Although the artifactual evidence occasionally creates more questions than it provides answers, archaeologists suspect that the site had been occupied for many centuries before a tragic massacre occurred there between 1325 and the mid-1400s. On the sides where the cliff did not provide natural protection, Native laborers had dug two fortification ditches 7 or 8 feet deep and over 1,000 feet long at the north and south ends of the village, which consisted of at least fifty-five earth lodges. They constructed a wooden palisade along the inner northern ditch, although no evidence has been found of a palisade along the outer ditch. The palisade that archaeologists found intact had been burned, presumably during the massacre or perhaps a prairie fire. The evidence shows that attackers shot their victims with stone-tipped arrows, caved in their heads with stone axes and wooden war clubs, and used stone knives to disfigure the bodies and scalp their victims. A mass grave 20 by 20 feet and a pile of bones 3 to 4 feet deep contained 486 mutilated bodies. Thus the completed fortifications and those under construction proved unsuccessful in protecting the inhabitants from Native attackers.

The historical record produced by European explorers who observed Mandan defenses corroborates the archaeological record. French military officer, explorer, and trapper Pierre Gaultier de Varennes et de La Vérendrye described a Mandan fort in 1738. He praised the organized village on the Heart River with 130 uniform cabins connected by clean, open streets. Surrounding the village was an "impregnable" timber palisade with four bastions along each wall and a ditch, over 15 feet deep and 13 to 18 feet wide, with a removable entryway. La Vérendrye suggested that Mandan fortifications varied only in size, noting that those "who saw one saw them all."

Fortifications were not unique to the Arikara and Mandan Nations. European explorers observed and described similar defensive works built by many other Great Plains tribes, including the Wichitas, Omahas, and Tawakonis. Each fort followed the same general pattern, with local modifications. Some forts included trenches in the interior of the palisades for the defense of women and children. Some used lodge poles and buffalo skins as part of the defenses. On the plains of Texas, the Tawakonis used naturally growing briars to slow their enemy's attack. In contrast, in the forested regions near the northern plains, the Blackfeet built small war lodges, camouflaged defensive refuges used by raiders being pursued. In the absence of trees or when time did not allow the construction of war lodges, Blackfeet raiders dug foxholes for defensive purposes. When pursued, Cheyenne raiders created impromptu stone breastworks to supplement naturally defensible positions. By the time of European arrival on the Great Plains, Indigenous peoples on the prairies had already been constructing fortifications for centuries. Indigenous fortifications are described in greater detail in chapter 1.

Spanish and Mexican Presidios

A century before representatives from American fur companies like Beckwourth established trading posts on the central and northern plains, other foreign powers left their mark on the plains. Spanish presidios—garrisoned, fortified frontier military outposts—were used to secure the nearly 1,800-mile Spanish borderlands (the northern border of New Spain), stretching from Florida to California. Some Spanish defenses on the plains were built to prevent intrusion by other nations, such as the French and the British.

Spanish presidios in Texas, New Mexico, and Arizona served a different purpose. On the southern plains, mounted

Indigenous warriors posed a threat to Spanish missions, towns, farms, ranches, and mines. The Spanish constructed presidios to defend their interests against Apaches and other Indigenous nations that were defending their homelands. Spanish soldiers stationed at these presidios escorted travelers and merchants, protected cattle and sheep herds from raiders, and demonstrated the perceived sovereignty of the Spanish crown over the region and its Native inhabitants. With these fortifications, like the Spanish presidios being constructed at the same time in Morocco, the term *presidio* connoted a bastion of Christian civilization within a hostile heathen land. In the eyes of Indigenous peoples, presidios represented further European intrusion onto their lands and into their lives.

The Spanish presidios on the southern plains included a military post at Santa Fe, New Mexico, and others on the Texas plains. A decade before the 1620 arrival of the *Mayflower* at Plymouth, Massachusetts, a presidio was built at Santa Fe within the Spanish borderlands. Though Pueblo resistance forced its abandonment in 1680, reconstructing the Santa Fe presidio in 1692 emboldened the Spaniards and strengthened their influence on the southern plains.

In 1716, in response to French attempts to colonize the Texas coast, Domingo Ramon constructed Presidio Dolores de los Tejas on the east bank of the Neches River near French Louisiana. Dolores was relocated once and abandoned in 1729 as the Spanish realized that the Natives of the region were peaceful and the immediate threats of French colonization waned. In 1718 Fray Antonio de Olivares organized the construction of Presidio San Antonio de Bexar to defend a nearby mission built two years earlier. This presidio, at the site of modern San Antonio, grew in population and power until it became the colonial capital in 1770. The Spanish presence on the southern plains expanded with the construction of Presidio Nuestra Senora de la Bahia del Espiritu Santo in 1722 and Presidio Nuestra Senora del Pilar de los Adaes in 1729. The garrisons at these presidios ranged from nine to over one hundred soldiers, depending on the circumstances and perceived needs.

Spanish plans for fortifications to the north never came to fruition. Pawnee and Otoe warriors, armed with French guns, thwarted Spanish efforts to construct a presidio on the Platte River in 1720. Natives frustrated Spanish hopes of expanding to the north again in 1758 when Comanches, Wichitas, and their allies overran the mission near Presidio de San Luis de las Amarillas. Although Spaniards occupied the presidio for another decade, the Indigenous peoples of the region had discouraged the Spanish from further fort construction in their area. Though the Spanish did not build additional forts on the plains, their influence remained.

Presidios were made of adobe or stone and patterned after Spain's military fortresses in Europe and Africa. Designed for defense against siege and cannon bombardment rather than for mounted hit-and-run attacks, presidios often included a walled enclosure with high towers for observation and embrasures through which cannons and small arms could be fired. Bastions projecting from walls allowed garrisoned troops to fire from several angles during a direct assault. None of these features proved of much use on the southern plains, where Comanche, Navajo, and Apache raiders targeted missions, villages, ranches, and mines rather than fortified presidios.

Spanish presidios of the southern plains started as small, isolated military outposts. Some lost their military importance over time and were abandoned, but Santa Fe and San Antonio grew into influential military and civilian communities. Both started with relatively few men. However, garrisoned soldiers brought wives and families, and Spanish settlers gravitated toward presidios for protection. Some Native nations saw the advantage of peaceful interaction and alliance with the Spanish. Nevertheless, Indigenous peoples universally loathed Spanish conquest, enslavement, and the coercive *encomienda* and *repartimiento* labor systems, which forced them to construct presidios and missions against their will. Spanish farmers, merchants, and ranchers, however, welcomed the security and the market for their products that presidios provided. Gradually, Spanish presidios of the southern plains significantly altered the human geography of the region.

Although relatively few and built principally in the seventeenth and eighteenth centuries, the Spanish presidios exerted a strong influence across much of the southern Great Plains—an influence that lasted beyond the nineteenth century. For example, when Gen. James Wilkinson, an American spy known by the Spaniards as Agent 13, tipped off the Spanish government that Meriwether Lewis and William Clark were leading a scientific and military expedition across the northern plains into contested territory in 1804, the governor of New Mexico, Fernando de Chacón, dispatched Spanish soldiers and their Comanche allies to intercept them. Four separate attempts to locate and arrest Lewis and Clark proved unsuccessful. In 1807, however, the Spanish learned that Zebulon Pike and his party had entered their territory on the southern plains, and they sent a force to apprehend the American interlopers. In February 1808 Spanish soldiers arrested Pike and his men at their makeshift fort on Rio Del Norte on the southwestern edge of the Great Plains, arriving with fifty dragoons and as many well-armed, mounted militia. Overwhelmed by the Spanish force, Pike had no alternative but to surrender his fort, men, and papers. The soldiers took Pike to Santa Fe, where officials interrogated him as an American spy. Soldiers then escorted Pike through Chihuahua and Spanish Texas before releasing him at Natchitoches, Louisiana. Spain's interest in protecting the Great Plains, as demonstrated by the Spaniards' construction of presidios and military presence, continued until events in Europe and America drove them out of North America when Mexico gained its independence.

By the time Mexico achieved independence from Spain in 1821, the presidios on the southern fringe of the Great Plains had deteriorated. Texas and New Mexico were so isolated from the Mexican heartland that the fledgling government paid them little attention. Mexican merchants continued their lucrative trade with Comanches and Kiowas of the southern plains, but in time, even these trade networks began to dry up. Additionally, a growing number of U.S. citizens moved into Mexican territory, leading to the Texas Revolution in 1836 and eventually war with the United States from 1846 to 1848. Despite the trading interests of Mexican merchants on the Great Plains, threats from Mexico's northern neighbor and increasingly violent encounters between Comanches and Mexicans prevented the Mexican government and private investors from building additional forts on the plains.

French Forts and Trading Posts

Like the Spanish, the French built forts on the Great Plains to strengthen their North American claims and gain access to the lucrative beaver fur and buffalo and deer hide trade. The French initially colonized the St. Lawrence River and Great Lakes drainages, eventually extending their influence across the Great Lakes and onto the Canadian Prairies. After 1682 they established a strong presence along the Mississippi River valley and its tributaries to the Gulf of Mexico. During the late seventeenth and early eighteenth centuries, when European nations scrambled to establish claims to North American territory, the French constructed fortifications along the St. Lawrence River, where their claims were undisputed by European rivals. French forts dotted the Great Lakes region of upstate New York and Vermont, as well as the Ohio, Mississippi, and Missouri River valleys from the modern-day state of Minnesota to Louisiana. The French built forts from the Gulf Coast of Texas to coastal Florida, and thence up the Atlantic Coast to the Carolinas. French forts varied from European-style fortresses to small trading entrepôts. By the early eighteenth century the French were constructing forts as trading posts on the northeastern borderlands of the Great Plains to form alliances with Indigenous traders and facilitate the lucrative fur trade.

In 1738 La Vérendrye constructed Fort La Reine as a fur-trading entrepôt on the Assiniboine River in what is now Manitoba on the northeastern plains. From this fort, French explorers searched for fur-rich waters to the north and west. The success of Fort La Reine led to the construction of other forts, including Fort Dauphin, Fort Bourbon, and Fort Pascoya to the north. At these forts, French trappers initiated trade with the Natives of the Upper Missouri River six decades before the Lewis and Clark Expedition. From Fort La Reine, La Vérendrye and his four sons explored the plains as far as the Rocky Mountains. After La Vérendrye's initial push onto the northern Great Plains, French trappers built two forts on the Saskatchewan River: Fort La Jonquière, the precise location of which is unknown and whose existence is sometimes disputed, and Fort de la Corne. These forts represented the westernmost reach of the French before the annexation of French Canada by the British at the end of the Seven Years' War. Although the French abandoned both Saskatchewan River forts within a decade of their construction, the London-based Hudson's Bay Company filled the void, building numerous trading houses and forts in the region.

Within a few years of the construction of French forts on the Saskatchewan River, other Frenchmen built a fort far to the south. In 1744, to accommodate trade with the powerful Kansa nation, François Coulon de Villiers took charge of newly constructed Fort de Cavagnial on the west shore of the Missouri River near modern-day Fort Leavenworth, Kansas. Like many other French forts, it doubled as a military outpost and a trading post, with as many as fifty military and civilian personnel on duty. Fort de Cavagnial facilitated the Great Plains fur trade until the French ceded Louisiana Territory to Spain in 1764. The effects of this fort were felt for decades. About forty years later, as Lewis and Clark passed along this stretch of the Missouri River, they were aware of the site of Fort de Cavagnial and noted that the area would make a suitable location for an agricultural colony.

The French forts of the central and northern Great Plains were different from the Spanish presidios to the south. Presidios were intended to demonstrate the strength of the Spanish and to intimidate or impress neighboring Native nations. Spanish government officials tried to maintain tight control over the presidios, determining the garrison strength and regulating their day-to-day affairs. By contrast, French forts were generally smaller and less heavily armed or defended, and they were intended to secure alliances with local Natives whom the French viewed as partners in the fur trade. Many Native nations welcomed the French as important trading allies—a source of firearms, ammunition, powder, iron traps, and other desirable trade goods—and many invited the French to build forts in or near their homelands for their own purposes. Natives who lacked access to European goods, which forts provided, were at a disadvantage in their conflicts with rival Indigenous peoples who had established trade with Europeans. French forts often had some minor defenses, such as wooden pickets with bastions at key locations. Both the French and their Indigenous partners recognized that the forts were designed not to withstand major resistance from local peoples but rather to serve as protection against the occasional raids mounted by rivals of their Indigenous allies.

Further, unlike the Spanish presidios, French forts were generally a result of government-sanctioned private enterprises and experienced much less government intrusion into their daily activities. Yet like the Spanish presidios, French entrepôts had an enormous impact on plains cultures. Through the trade that forts facilitated, Native peoples of the Great Plains had greater access to guns, traps, and other goods, drastically altering their traditional culture. Native nations that lived in closest proximity to French forts gained a substantial military advantage over their rivals. The nature of warfare changed, as firearms escalated the violence of formerly small-scale skirmishes, and horses continued to increase mobility and quick-strike potential. Moreover, the fauna of the Great Plains experienced significant stress as beavers and other fur-bearing animals were trapped out of rivers and streams. Native hunters armed with guns harvested greater numbers of bison and initiated the decline of their herds on the plains.

British Forts and Trading Posts

During the eighteenth century the British, like the French, hoped to enlarge their presence in North America. The two nations competed for control of fishing and furs from the Atlantic Coast to the Ohio River valley. To strengthen their claims and intimidate their rivals, the British also built forts. In the early years of competition, the Great Plains were of secondary concern to the French and the British, since their interests lay primarily from the Mississippi region to the Appalachians and Great Lakes. In 1713 the British crown granted the Hudson's Bay Company (HBC) a fur trade monopoly for all the streams within the Hudson Bay drainage. Meanwhile, France maintained exclusive fur trade rights in the St. Lawrence and Mississippi River drainages. From these bases, French and English trappers began interacting with Natives who called the plains home.

It is not surprising that eventually the British, like the French, established trading houses and forts on the plains to facilitate trade with Native nations. After the British government seized control of North America from the French in 1763, the HBC established hundreds of trading houses across North America in an unprecedented expansion of its fur trade empire. By the mid-1700s these trading houses, often called forts, though they were little more than trading posts, connected British executives with nearly every Native nation, including those living on the Great Plains and Canadian Prairies.

For example, in 1774 the HBC established Cumberland House on the Saskatchewan River on the Canadian plains. Within a few years, Cumberland House became one of the most important trading outposts in Canada. Its location proved ideal for the fur trade. The Saskatchewan River flowed into Lake Winnipeg, linked by river to York Factory at the confluence of the Hayes River, the company's northern headquarters on Hudson Bay. Additionally, the Saskatchewan River facilitated canoe commerce with people to the north and west as far as the Rocky Mountains and the Continental Divide. Cumberland House was constructed in the heart of a region teeming with beavers and other animals whose skins were in great demand. Further, the Cree Nation, who lived in the area, became an important trade partner. A hub in the interaction between the HBC officials and its British, French, Métis, and Native agents and partners, Cumberland House was only one of hundreds of trading houses built by the HBC.

Rival companies desired to acquire the fur resources of the plains by building forts (see chapter 2). British rivalry on the Great Plains increased with the establishment of the North West

Company (NWC) in the late 1770s to challenge the HBC. North West Company founders in Montreal hoped to break the HBC stranglehold by garnering the fur resources west of the HBC's royal charter. At first their interests lay in the northernmost regions of Canada. Explorers such as Alexander Mackenzie blazed trails to the Arctic and Pacific Oceans. Later, explorers like David Thompson and Simon Fraser explored to the south, crossing the Canadian Prairies and Canadian Rocky Mountains. The NWC built trading houses patterned after those of the HBC. Most of these posts were situated along rivers in mountain valleys along the edge of the Great Plains. For instance, NWC employees David Thompson and James McMillan built Flathead Post (Saleesh House) in western Montana. This post facilitated trade with the Flathead/Salish Nation and soon became a crossroads of contact between Native trappers and hunters and British officials of the NWC. As the NWC expanded, it came into conflict with the HBC. After several violent encounters in the 1810s, the two companies merged in 1821 under the name of the Hudson's Bay Company. The combined resources of these two powerful firms proved a significant barrier to the development of fur trade and exploitation of the Great Plains by U.S. interests, but it did not stop them from trying.

U.S. Forts

On July 4, 1803, Thomas Jefferson announced the purchase of the Louisiana Territory's rights of discovery from France for $15 million, giving the United States claim to the Missouri River drainage, which included most of the Great Plains. Congress ratified the April 20 signing of the Louisiana Purchase Treaty on October 20. Jefferson soon asked Meriwether Lewis to lead a scientific expedition to follow the Missouri River to its headwaters and search for a Northwest Passage—a convenient river route across North America for the purposes of commerce.

Lewis was assigned to establish peaceful relations with Natives and seek resources for expanding the fledgling American fur trade. Lewis invited William Clark to accompany him as co-commander of the expedition.

Lewis and Clark's venture along the Missouri River took them across the heartland of the Great Plains. During the winter of 1804–5, while camped on the shore of the Missouri River in present-day North Dakota, they built Fort Mandan, a triangular stockade made of lumber from nearby cottonwood trees, close to Mandan and Hidatsa villages. Members of these nations cautiously engaged in trade with the Americans, but the Hidatsas did not want to jeopardize their ongoing partnership with the British. While wintering at Fort Mandan, Lewis and Clark met and enlisted a Shoshone teenager, Sacagawea, and her NWC husband, Toussaint Charbonneau, as guides and interpreters. Although Fort Mandan represented one of the first U.S. forts on the Great Plains, it did not survive even until the end of Lewis and Clark's expedition. When they returned in 1806, it had been burned to the ground. As Lewis and Clark traveled west, they noted other suitable sites for forts and trading posts.

From the time of Lewis and Clark's return until the 1830s, American fort construction on the Great Plains involved the work of individuals and private trapping companies, and the forts were primarily small trading posts of wood or adobe. Expedition members and others returned west to enter into commerce with the plains' Indigenous inhabitants. In 1809 Manuel Lisa founded the Missouri Fur Company. Within a year 150 company employees embarked on an exploration and trade mission with supplies to build several trading posts. The first was Fort Lisa at the mouth of the Bighorn River, where they wintered, followed by Three Forks Post at the confluence of the Jefferson and Madison Rivers. The Blackfeet Confederacy drove the Americans away, forcing the abandonment of Three

Forks Post. The Blackfeet objected to American intrusion into their sovereign territory and opposed American trade with their Shoshone, Crow, Flathead, and Nez Perce rivals. The struggles of the Missouri Fur Company expedition demonstrated the challenges of entering the fur trade business and constructing forts on the Great Plains.

Trying to break into the lucrative fur trade from different directions, agents from John Jacob Astor's American Fur Company traveled by sea and by land to the Pacific Northwest. They constructed Fort Astoria near the mouth of the Columbia River on the Pacific Coast. Seeking new waters in which to trap, his agents explored unfamiliar territory between the Rocky Mountains and the Mississippi River, finding the South Pass through the Rockies. They were not alone in their quest to fully exploit the resources of the Far West and the Great Plains. Within a few years of the construction of Fort Astoria, William Ashley and Andrew Henry established the precursor of the Rocky Mountain Fur Company in St. Louis and began to build outposts in the West. However, in 1822 an innovation developed by Ashley and Henry reduced the need for forts on the Great Plains and in the Rocky Mountains. Instead of permanent outposts, the maintenance of which could be expensive and hazardous, the Rocky Mountain Fur Company sponsored annual rendezvous from 1825 until 1840, with large supply trains carrying necessary goods west and furs east.

By the mid-1830s the heyday of trapping had passed, and American fort construction shifted from building fur trade outposts to serving the needs of the growing numbers of settlers traveling to the American West. A handful of forts, such as Bent's Fort, had few difficulties repurposing for changing times and the emigrant trade. By 1846, the year of Susan Magoffin's visit, merchants had been traveling the Santa Fe Trail for over two decades, basking in the relative comforts of Bent's Fort.

Not all forts from the fur-trading era were equally flexible, and many were abandoned, burned, washed away by shifting rivers, or otherwise reclaimed by nature. They were sometimes replaced by new forts in locations that made sense for the changing needs of the time—at river fords, in areas where Natives and overland travelers might meet, or at other strategic crossroads. Over the Santa Fe Trail's sixty-year history, scores of forts were built, relocated, and abandoned along the trail's various routes. Similarly, forts were constructed on the plains to facilitate travel along the Oregon, California, and Mormon Pioneer trails. Forty-niners and other pioneers knew they could make needed wagon repairs, resupply their depleted stores, and seek refuge at Forts Leavenworth, Kearny, Laramie, and Bridger while crossing the plains of modern-day Kansas, Nebraska, and Wyoming. Chapter 3 highlights these overland emporiums in greater depth.

As national borders became established, the U.S. government strengthened its military presence on the plains, and the term *fort* began to have military connotations. Along with protecting pioneer trails, soldiers stationed at forts such as Randall, on the Missouri River on the present-day border of South Dakota and Nebraska, protected telegraph lines, stagecoach stations, and other American interests. They also served as the launching point of various military offensives against Native peoples. Great Plains forts, such as Fort Leavenworth in Kansas and Fort Gibson in Indian Territory, served as recruiting and training areas during the Civil War for Union and Confederate troops, respectively. Fort Gibson was occupied at various times during the Civil War by Union troops but was not the site of any major battles.

Following the Civil War, soldiers garrisoned in forts supported the construction of the transcontinental railroad and its spurs and waged the Indian Wars of the 1870s and 1880s. Forts were often connected to the east by railroad lines, which diminished the isolation of the soldiers garrisoned on the plains.

Linking forts by railroad facilitated the movement of troops and goods. The presence of forts frustrated Native resistance to colonization, dispossession, and removal. Forts proved instrumental in the government's efforts to force Indigenous Americans onto reservations and aided efforts to destroy Native self-sufficiency by exterminating the bison herds. In the reservation era, places like Fort Niobrara, constructed in 1880 on the Niobrara River in present-day Nebraska, became distribution centers for supplies to regional Indian agencies. From these forts, soldiers also worked to prevent cattle rustling, uphold (and sometimes undermine) Indians' rights, maintain law and order, and give the new inhabitants peace of mind.

Changing conditions around the turn of the century changed the purpose and nature of forts once again. The tragic 1890 massacre at Wounded Knee Creek, wherein U.S. cavalry killed between two hundred and three hundred Lakota men, women, and children; the emphasis on eradicating Native cultures through assimilation and acculturation; and the confinement of most Indigenous and First Peoples on reservations and reserves diminished U.S. and Canadian interests in maintaining many of the forts of the Great Plains and Canadian Prairies. Some forts were simply abandoned. Others were retooled to serve different purposes, primarily military recruiting, staging, and training. Instead of small forts dotting the plains, resources were pooled into larger installations. Fort Leavenworth, for example, expanded into thousands of buildings and barracks across 5,600 acres. Through most of the twentieth century Fort Leavenworth has fulfilled multiple purposes, among them housing a maximum-security prison for the U.S. Department of Defense and serving as the home of the U.S. Army Combined Arms Center and the base of the National Guard's Thirty-Fifth Infantry Division. Chapter 4 focuses on the military forts that dotted the Great Plains and Canadian Prairies, while chapter 5 provides greater detail on the fur-trading posts of the Canadian Prairies.

From the time Indigenous peoples constructed their first fortifications against their enemies to the arrival of European and American fort builders, Great Plains forts have played a central role in the story of the prairies. Forts were shaped by, and have shaped, the physical and human geography of the region. Like the human actors in the story of the plains, forts have come and gone, each one leaving an indelible mark on the land and the people. Today most forts have deteriorated or been destroyed, some have been restored, and a handful remain operational.

GREAT PLAINS FORTS

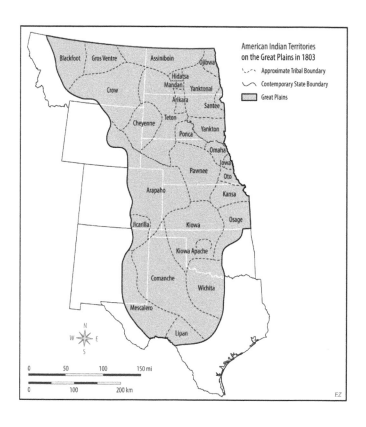

Fig. 4. *American Indian Territories on the Great Plains in 1803.* Map by Ezra J. Zeitler. From David J. Wishart, *Great Plains Indians* (Lincoln: University of Nebraska Press, 2016), 33.

CHAPTER ONE

Indigenous Fortifications

Archaeologists investigating an ancient Indigenous village on the east bank of the Missouri River in central South Dakota in 1978 made a shocking discovery: a mass grave containing the remains of at least 486 men, women, and children who had suffered a violent death. Their scalped, mutilated, decapitated, and dismembered bodies filled the village's defensive ditch with bones piled 3 feet deep. How had these inhabitants of the area met their doom, which archaeologists determined occurred sometime around 1325 AD? Other archaeological evidence at the site painted a grisly picture of the story behind the murders.

Around 1100 AD a Native village thrived along the Missouri River at a site now located within the Crow Creek Indian Reservation in present-day South Dakota. Streams to the south and west provided a steady water supply for this farming village, and its population grew over the decades. Changes occurred around 1300 as climatic forces and other factors caused food shortages and starvation. The famine led to conflict between the Crow Creek village and similar communities along the Missouri. At some point before the massacre, the inhabitants of Crow Creek began to build defensive fortifications around their village. They used the natural defenses provided by the creeks to the south and west and began to fortify the north side of the village. Their defenses featured both inner and outer palisades. The inner walls were fronted by a defensive ditch 1,250 feet long, varying from 15 to 50 feet wide and 6 to 12 feet deep. After experiencing an extended period of peace and expansion, Middle Missouri residents at Crow Creek found it necessary to build a second, much larger defensive system around their expanded village, with twelve bastions on the outer stockade and a new ditch 12 feet wide and 6 feet deep.

Evidence suggests that rival Native attackers breached the defenses and massacred the villagers, possibly while they tried to augment their fortifications. The invaders burned the homes, granaries, and other structures, filling one of the fortification ditches with the scalped, mutilated, and dismembered bodies of their victims. The practice of mutilating enemy bodies stemmed from the notion that if one met these same enemies in the next life, they would lack their sight, hearing, reproductive organs, arms, and so forth, rendering them defenseless and incapable of doing one harm. The Crow Creek Massacre reveals that the elaborate defenses sometimes constructed by the Indigenous inhabitants of the Great Plains did not always successfully ward off enemy attacks from without or resolve the vulnerabilities of internal revolt. Although an extreme example, the Crow Creek Massacre highlights the dangers Great Plains peoples faced and the scale of the combat and destruction that could take place.

In this chapter, we explore the fortifications constructed by the Indigenous peoples who lived on the Great Plains to protect themselves from a fate like that of the Crow Creek village. We begin by considering the evolving conditions on the plains that led to distinct types of fortifications. We describe Mandan, Hidatsa, Arikara, and Wichita defenses on the eastern plains and offer examples of defensive sites and refuge strongholds on the western high plains.

Tribal Warfare and Defenses

The Great Plains has a rich Indigenous history. Native nations of the Great Plains region include Arapahos, Arikaras, Assiniboines, Blackfeet, Caddos, Cheyennes, Comanches, Crows, Dakotas, Gros Ventres/Atsinas, Hidatsas, Ioways, Kaws, Kiowas, Kitsai, Lakotas, Lipans, Mandans, Métis, Missourias, Nakotas, Omahas, Osages, Otoes, Pawnees, Plains Apaches, Plains Crees, Plains Ojibwas, Poncas, Quapaws, Salteaux, Sarcees, Stoneys, Teyas, Tonkawas, Tsuut'inas, and Wichitas and Affiliated Tribes (Wacos, Tawakonis, Kichai, Taovayas, and Yscanis).

Archaeological evidence reveals little regarding Indigenous warfare on the Great Plains before 1000 AD, when people living on the plains generally dwelled in small, unfortified communities as peaceful horticulturists. Between 1100 and 1300, however, farmers joined together to form larger, fortified communities to protect themselves from the increasing severity of raids from other Native groups. While some scholars have posited that colonial contact augmented the scale and intensity of intertribal warfare, archaeological data verify that high-casualty intertribal warfare existed in various Great Plains locales for hundreds of years before colonial contact, and Indigenous peoples enacted defensive measures to counter these militaristic threats from rival Native nations.

Indigenous fortifications throughout the Great Plains reveal several commonalities. Over the centuries, Natives employed several types of fortifications to defend themselves from assailants, as tribal nations competed over territory and resources. Indigenous peoples selected naturally defensible locations for their settlements whenever possible. Otherwise, they constructed a variety of defensive structures to fortify themselves against attack, whether from feuding, revenge killing, or full-scale warfare. The archaeological record suggests that most

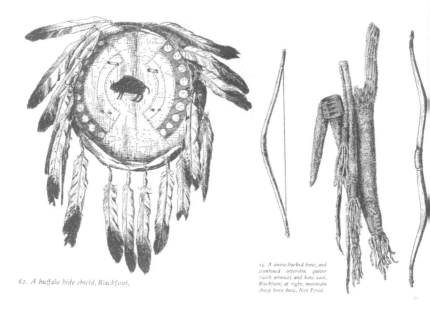

62. *A buffalo hide shield, Blackfoot.*

13. *A sinew-backed bow, and combined otterskin quiver (with arrows) and bow case, Blackfoot; at right, mountain sheep horn bow, Nez Percé.*

Fig. 5. Buffalo hide shield and Plains Indian weaponry. From Robert H. Lowie, *Indians of the Plains* (Lincoln: University of Nebraska Press, 1982), 71, 76.

Indigenous societies on the Great Plains experienced at least one feud or war every decade. Small groups with great mobility had fewer incidents of violence and built fewer fortifications than more populous, sedentary villagers.

Fortifications protected communities or marked edges of territorial boundaries. Defensive systems usually fell into one of three types: fortifications, defensive sites, or refuge strongholds. Fortifications included large-scale architecture and usually had a combination of a barrier-wall system, gates, bastions, and ditches, with a weapons system suitable for defense. Archaeologists categorize sites without these substantial architectural features but with some measure of defenses as protection sites rather than fortifications. A third form of defense, a refuge stronghold, consisted of a hastily constructed shelter intended for short-term safety.

Native warfare involved a variety of weapons. Rocks thrown by hand or sling, war club maces, lances or javelins, atlatls (spear-throwing boards and thongs), stone battle-axes, knives, and bows and arrows had varying effective ranges of 30 to 300 feet in pitched battles or surprise raids. Battle-axes worked well at close range; a sapling served as a long handle to which was attached a grooved stone head pointed at both ends, secured together by rawhide bands. Warriors threw lances or used them in hand-to-hand combat once outer defenses had been breached. After 1200 AD the bow and arrow functioned as the preeminent and most effective weapon for hunting and warfare. Bows could be long or short, depending on their purpose, and propelled arrows with deadly force against animals or enemies. Natives usually made bows out of wood, but some used elk antler or bighorn sheep horn.

Indigenous peoples such as the Mandans, Osages, and Wichitas constructed shields of woven wicker or the more impenetrable bison leather. Buffalo-hide shields, made by stretching a wet hide over a wooden frame and allowing it to dry taut and hard, offered excellent protection from arrows and spears but later proved less effective against lead balls from musket fire. Pawnees, Padoucas (Apaches or Comanches), Caddos, and Taovayas made armor and breastplates from double layers of elk leather with sand quilted or glued between the layers. They also made heavy bison-hide head coverings, some decorated with feathers or buffalo horns.

The acquisition of horses during the seventeenth century led to further innovations for Indigenous peoples, including their warfare and defenses. Horses brought wealth and security, and their adoption by some tribes dramatically transformed the

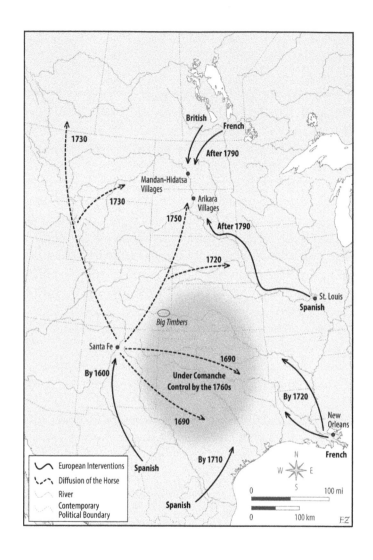

Fig. 6. *Spread of the horse throughout the Great Plains.* Map by Ezra J. Zeitler. From David J. Wishart, *Great Plains Indians* (Lincoln: University of Nebraska Press, 2016), 17.

economies of nomadic and semisedentary groups. Indigenous hunters on horseback could obtain enough bison in spring and fall hunts to sustain them year-round. Lodge sizes grew, since horses could pull more on the travois than a person or dog could. Horse-mounted buffalo hunting affected Native culture and enhanced and increased participation in the Sun Dance, the Buffalo Bull Dance, and other ceremonies associated with the buffalo. Warrior societies expanded after horse technology arrived. Greater mobility and range escalated tribal conflict on the plains. Mounted troops either abandoned or diminished the size of the shields used in warfare. Native rock art from Alberta to Texas depicts armored horses and equestrian warriors such as the Comanches and Crows, who made leather armor to protect their horses' heads, necks, and chests from lances and arrows. Contestation over hunting grounds and food resources increased as mounted warriors conquered their neighbors and expanded their territory at the expense of other Indigenous peoples. Raiding intensified, as did the enslavement and captivity of women and children to replace tribal members lost in battle. The enslavers often adopted captives who lived through the first few weeks of the ordeal. Sedentary villagers faced three options: fortify, fight, or flee. The majority chose to fortify first, building ever more elaborate and extensive fortifications for protection.

Early fortifications were constructed from interlaced willows or thorns, felled trees, stacked rocks, and other structures used for temporary or permanent defense. Over time, these simple defenses evolved into more elaborate wall structures made of earth, timber, and stone. Walls were made from natural or shaped stones, adobe, or baked bricks or were earthen-bank ramparts. Residents dug moats and trenches around the outer perimeter, sometimes filling them with water, to increase the defensive strength. Behind the moat, a wall curtain or surrounding wall, built by placing large timbers on end at regular intervals, proved an effective deterrent to the attackers' weapons and sallies. Workers sometimes partially covered the wall with earth, plants, adobe, or hides that concealed the interior. Moats discouraged enemies from undermining the curtained wall. These enceintes (surrounding barriers or enclosures) usually consisted of a defensible entryway or gate and bastions to defend the perimeter palisade. The gate remained the most vulnerable point in walled and moated villages. Indigenous peoples innovated using various forms of baffled, screened, and flanked gates to defend their towns from attack. These gates usually overlapped the curtained defenses of ditches, ramparts, and palisades and included hide coverings or daubed adobe over wood for additional strength and forced attackers to expose their flanks and rear to the defenders' fire.

Along with defended gates, V-sectioned ditches more than 3 feet deep and 10 feet wide at ground level, backed by a barrier, proved a formidable obstacle to direct assault. The palisade behind the ditch often included hide coverings or daubed wooden stakes to protect the structure against enemy attack and from catching on fire. The regularly spaced bastions—along with loopholes through which the villagers discharged projectiles—provided overlapping fields of fire against attackers and mutual cover for other bastions. These elevated platforms also provided greater visibility and locations from which archers could rain down arrows on the invaders and those trying to breach the wall.

Mandan and Hidatsa Defenses

Around 1800 AD Mandan chief Sheheke-shote (or Big White Coyote) and his wife, Yellow Corn, climbed to the top of a rise overlooking his Mitutanka (Matootonha) village along the Knife River near its confluence with the Missouri. The Mandan couple gazed out on Matootonha's defenses. Inaccessible from two sides, the village was fortified with ditch defenses and a picket palisade of timbers a foot in diameter set in the ground and rising 18 feet high. The gaps between the timbers allowed for defenders to fire guns or shoot arrows at invaders while protected by a trench to screen their bodies from enemy attack. The gregarious and slightly rotund leader was on good terms with Black Cat, the leader of the neighboring Mandan village of Rooptahee, but the Mandans never knew when rival enemies from the east and south might attack.

Archaeologists postulate that Siouan-speaking Mandans (who called themselves Numangkaki, meaning "People of the First Man") settled on the Great Plains along the Heart River around 1000 AD. Matrilineal clans brought order to family relationships, with a clan comprising all the women and children in a family. Clans cared for one another and used sacred bundles in performing ceremonies such as the Okipa to remember the story of Lone Man's creation of the Mandan world and his gifting of the animals to the Mandans. Ceremonies were held to ensure successful hunts and plentiful harvests. Villagers selected as their leaders two men—a diplomat and a warrior—from the general council of each autonomous village.

People often think of stereotyped images of the Plains Indians as equestrian nomads living in buffalo-hide tepees. Before the dispersal of Spanish horses following the Pueblo Revolt of 1680, however, Indigenous nations on the northeastern Great Plains typically were sedentary, living in villages along the rivers. These farmers and hunters of the Upper Missouri River valley cleared brush, willows, and cottonwoods from their fields. Women used bison scapula hoes and fire-hardened digging sticks to cultivate corn, beans, squash, and sunflowers on the alluvial flats of the Missouri. The floodplain proved unsuitable for permanent dwelling but ideal for growing crops in tended gardens. Fish from the river, mammals that came to drink, abundant berries, and bison harvested from the plains complemented the crops from their fields to provide a balanced diet.

River valleys carved into the plains served as an arboreal oasis, with hardwoods such as elm, ash, oak, box elder, and bur oak. These trees proved ideal for use as firewood for cooking and warmth, poles for home construction, and timber for defensive palisades surrounding the villages, usually located on terraced rims above the floodplain or on the prairie bluffs above the river. Whenever possible, Mandans situated their villages at the points of promontories, defensible positions against enemies approaching from the plains. They built four-pole earth lodges oriented in the cardinal directions, with a second row of posts running around the perimeter of the floor.

Sometime after 1400 AD wars among villages over resources caused the Mandans to begin to construct defensive moats and log stockades around their villages. These fortified towns expanded in size and population until the 1500s, when drought decreased the amount of arable land. The number of villages fluctuated between six and thirteen, and village size also varied, depending on how available resources and climate change affected population numbers. Around 1500 the Mandans adapted their rectangular earth lodges into a circular shape, perhaps influenced by their new neighbors, the Arikara to the south and the Hidatsa to the north, whom they had invited to settle along Missouri River tributaries.

By the 1700s three Mandan subgroups lived in fortified villages along the Heart River near its confluence with the Missouri. In each village, an inner circle of lodges faced an open plaza about 150 feet in diameter. In the plaza center stood a barrel-like holy place made of split cottonwood planks enclosing a red-painted cedar pole. This monument symbolized the Mandan hero Lone Man and represented the structure that, according to legend, he had built to save the Mandan people during a primordial flood. It is not surprising that these villages attracted the attention of European and American explorers as they ventured west.

In early December 1738 French explorer Pierre Gaultier de Varennes et de La Vérendrye and his sons visited an earth lodge village close to present-day Bismarck, North Dakota. He marveled at the orderliness of the layout of the village, which comprised 130 uniform lodges, and noted the clean and well-kept streets. The villagers divided their large, spacious lodges into several apartments with thick planks and left nothing lying about, making their beds and hanging their baggage neatly on posts. La Vérendrye chronicled the town's extensive fortifications in his journal: "The ramparts are smooth and wide; the palisade is supported on cross pieces mortised into posts fifteen feet apart with a lining. For this purpose, they use green hides fastened only at the top in places where they are needed." He marveled at the village's defensive ditch, 15 feet deep and 15 feet wide, with four bastions along each wall, and reflected that the fort could be entered only by climbing steps or posts, "which can be removed when threatened by an enemy. If all their forts are alike, they may be called impregnable to Indians." Yet despite these precautions and La Vérendrye's glowing report, in 1779 two thousand Lakotas attacked and breached a fortified Mandan village like this one, killing all the inhabitants.

Before the 1700s the Indigenous peoples inhabiting villages on the Upper Missouri ruled the plains. After the dispersal of horses, their dominance was immediately challenged. Lakotas, Nakotas, and Dakotas adopted horse culture, leaving behind the forested Great Lakes region, and expanded their territory westward onto the grasslands of the northern plains. In their interactions with Upper Missouri village dwellers, they engaged in a blend of friendly trading, aggressive raiding, and outright warfare to expand their influence, procure material goods, and weaken their enemies. When a smallpox epidemic struck the earth lodge peoples in 1780–82, the Lakotas ramped up their attacks on the weakened communities, launching mounted war parties to raid sedentary villages. The expansion of the Lakotas and other equestrian, bison-hunting cultures had a detrimental impact on villagers living along the Upper Missouri. By the nineteenth century the Lakotas had become the dominant force along the Missouri River in the Dakotas.

Sometime after La Vérendrye's visit, the Mandans moved north to the mouth of Knife River (near present-day Stanton, North Dakota), adjacent to their Hidatsa friends, to put some distance between themselves and their powerful mounted Lakota adversaries to the south. The Mandans typically chose to situate their villages on naturally defended Missouri River bluffs like the Knife River site, where the high bluff protected one side. They took other measures to protect the vulnerable sides, where they constructed ditches, palisades, and pickets to discourage enemy attacks.

These fortified Mandan villages, like Sheheke-shote's Matootonha, functioned as defensive strongholds and epicenters of an extensive trade network on the northern plains. Mandan generosity and hospitality brought Native guests from many nations to their villages. Later, as Europeans and Americans entered the Great Plains trade network, they also visited the Mandan villages. The Mandans held seasonal trading fairs, where they exchanged dried vegetables for bison robes and other goods from the Great Plains, Great Lakes, and even Europe. European visitors wrote accounts and made artistic renditions of Mandan fortifications. Visiting artists such as George Catlin and Swiss watercolorist Karl Bodmer captured the expansive Mandan trading and ceremonial community plazas in their drawings and paintings.

Fig. 7. *Bird's Eye View of the Mandan Village, 1800 Miles above St. Louis* by George Catlin. Note the palisade wall facing the prairie. Courtesy Smithsonian American Art Museum.

In 1798, six decades after La Vérendrye's visit, North West Company trader, explorer, and cartographer David Thompson traveled to a heavily fortified Mandan settlement and wrote a vivid description: "They were all strongly stockaded with posts of wood of ten to twelve inches in diameter; about two feet in the ground and ten feet above it, with numerous holes to fire through; they went round the village, in some places close to the houses; there were two doorways to each of the stockades, on opposite sides; they are shut up when required, with logs of wood." Even these defenses sometimes proved insufficient. When Lewis and Clark explored the Missouri River in 1803, they found several abandoned villages.

The Hidatsas built villages along the Missouri River to the north of their Mandan allies, some with fortifications like those used by their neighbors to the south. Archaeological work conducted in 2018 at the Molander site (about 11 miles south of present-day Washburn, North Dakota) revealed that it was a hub of activity of one of the three Hidatsa tribal divisions that had arrived at the Missouri River by 1600. Located on the west bank of the Missouri in northeastern Oliver County, North Dakota, Molander had two settlements where Hidatsas lived between 1735 and 1765. Defensive structures surrounded the 5.2 acres of the upper or western village, the larger of the two. The lower or eastern village lacked similar fortifications. Excavations unearthed stone and bone tools, flakes, pottery sherds, floral and faunal remains, trade goods, and other materials that shed light on the Hidatsas' material culture. And the archaeological work provided excellent insight into earth lodge construction. Moreover, the excavations revealed the extensive efforts the Hidatsas undertook to fortify their village. The defensive structures remain one of the most prominent visible features at the site and represent one of the best-preserved Indigenous fortifications on the northern plains.

The village included both natural and human-produced defenses, with a deep ravine and a defensive ditch completely encircling the lodge homes. The fortification ditch measured roughly 5 feet wide at the bottom, 12 feet wide at the top, 5 feet deep, and 1,445 feet long. Hidatsa workers excavated 47,674.8 cubic feet of earth during construction of the ditch. Archaeologists calculated that with the excavation productivity of 17.66 cubic feet a day per person, excavating and constructing the defenses would have required 3,596 person-days, a monumental communal accomplishment for a village of this size. Archaeologists based their calculations on twenty-five excavated loads of 0.71 cubic feet (44.1 pounds) each, or one large basket load of dirt every twenty minutes for eight hours. With villages such as Big Hidatsa containing over one hundred lodges and having log palisades surrounding the perimeter, home and fortification architecture also required a great deal of lumber.

Hidatsa workers built up an earthen terrace with the dirt excavated from the ditch. They placed their subterranean storage pits in a line along the interior wall of the fortification ditch and terrace, and they located their trash dump pits outside the enclosed village. Hidatsa architects cut a defensible bench into the side of the ravine. They erected eight bastions on the ditch terrace, several of which corresponded with natural ridges that the builders incorporated into their defensive design. Builders strengthened the ditch, terrace, and bastion complex with an interior log palisade that stretched 1,883 feet and required 1,780 or more posts at least 10 feet long. Workers harvested and transported lumber, erected the picket framework, and collected, prepared, and attached the rawhide covering to enclose the village wall. Community leaders and residents devoted considerable time, labor, and capital to completing an elaborate town defense. Analysis of artifacts and aerial photogrammetry of this well-preserved system illuminates a more comprehensive understanding of Indigenous cultural landscapes and offers insights into Hidatsa community projects, leadership, mobility, and warfare. Of importance, the efforts made by Hidatsa villagers at the Molander site represent similar defense mechanisms at other fortified village sites like Boley, Huff, Larson, and Double Ditch.

The Awaxawi Hidatsas at Molander, roughly equidistant between the Knife and Heart Rivers, developed close economic ties with the Mandans at Heart River and shared intimate cultural ties with the Hidatsas at Knife River. The historical record surrounding the Molander site corroborates the archaeological findings. Explorer William Clark described the site in his journal entry on October 23, 1804, as the expedition "passed an old [village] of a Band of Me ne tarres Called Mah har ha [an English interpretation of the Mandan term *wąxá·xa* and Hidatsa word *awaxáʔwi*, meaning 'spread out place'] where they lived 40 year ago [i.e., 1764] on the L. S. [larboard or left side of the boat]." Clark marked the site of the village on his Missouri route map in the bend immediately below the expedition's October 23 camp. As Clark noted, the Hidatsas abandoned the Molander site shortly after the French and Indian War and joined the other two Hidatsa divisions, establishing Amahami village at the confluence of the Knife and Missouri Rivers by 1786. Explorer Alexander Henry noted that the Hidatsa villagers shared a language similar to the Mandans and that from their proximity had acquired Mandan manners and customs, although they continued to live separately in one of their five main settlements.

Unfortunately for the Mandans and Hidatsas, things did not go smoothly at Knife River, despite their generosity, hospitality, and friendship with Americans. In 1837 a devastating smallpox epidemic killed many of the residents, leaving fewer than two hundred survivors. Their fortifications were useless without adequate defenders, rendering them vulnerable to attack from Indigenous neighbors. As a new defensive measure, they moved up the Missouri and established Like-a-Fishhook Village, which became an important trading and administration center for the region after 1845.

Consisting of earth lodges and log cabins, Like-a-Fishhook had a fine central plaza, with the sacred Lone Man cedar occupying its revered place in the center of town. Next to the plaza was a ceremonial lodge used for community gatherings and ceremonies like the Okipa. As Lakota raiders were a continual threat, Hidatsa and Mandan workers constructed a palisade around the village, with wooden posts as close together as their shapes allowed and too high for enemies to climb easily. Digging a ditch around the palisade, they piled dirt about 3 feet high against the wall and dug another ditch on the inside of the fence. Projecting outward beyond the line of the wall were embedded bastions, on which they built a platform resting on four posts, accessible by a ladder. Loopholes above and below the platform allowed defenders to shoot through the palisade and defend the village with arrows and bullets. After hundreds of years of practice, these fortification efforts must have seemed commonplace necessities by the allied Hidatsa and Mandan communities.

Arikara and Wichita Defenses

Caddoan-speaking peoples arrived on the plains around 1000 AD. They adapted to their surroundings and soon inhabited the Great Plains from what is now South Dakota to Texas. In addition to the Arikaras in the Dakotas, the Pawnees inhabited Nebraska and Kansas, and the Wichitas and their relatives lived in communities stretching from Kansas to Texas. The Arikaras became experts at earth lodge construction, with Arikara women training the Omahas, Oto-Missourias, and other tribes in the art.

Arikaras fortified their earth lodge villages in the Dakotas using soil and water. At the Sheyenne-Cheyenne archaeological site (12 miles southeast of present-day Lisbon, North Dakota), Arikaras and Cheyennes constructed a village on top of a steep river terrace overlooking a former course of the Cheyenne River. With the steep riverbank protecting them from a southern attack, they surrounded the exposed perimeter of their village with a moat more than 6 feet deep and 10 feet wide. They also cast up earthen embankments to give the defending force the distinct advantage that came with an elevated position. Nevertheless, these measures did not always prevent enemy incursion. Sometime during the mid-eighteenth century, Chippewa or Assiniboine raiders burned this village to the ground, forcing its abandonment.

Written records from early trappers corroborate the evidence discovered by archaeologists at the Sheyenne-Cheyenne site. In

1795 French trader Jean Baptiste Trudeau entered an Arikara fort. The Caddoan-speaking Arikaras informed him that their spy network had uncovered a Lakota plot to send five hundred warriors against their village. Trudeau noted in his journal that the Arikaras fortified their village by placing palisades 5 feet high, which they had reinforced with earth. "The fort is constructed in the following manner: All around their village they drive into the ground heavy forked stakes, standing from four to five feet high and from fifteen to twenty feet apart. Upon these are placed cross-pieces as thick as one's thigh; next they place poles of willow or cottonwood, as thick as one's leg, resting on cross-pieces and very close together." He recounted how the Arikaras piled brush against these 5-foot-high poles before they covered them "with an embankment of earth two feet thick; in this way, the height of the poles would prevent the scaling of the fort by the enemy, while the well-packed earth protects those within from their balls and arrows."

Arikaras also occupied a village on the Missouri River, known as the Larson site, between 1750 and 1785. They fortified their town of twenty-nine earth lodges with two ditches backed by palisades. These fortifications did not discourage a raiding party, possibly made up of Lakota warriors, from attacking in 1785. When invaders penetrated the outer defenses during the assault, Arikara women, being experienced earthmovers, frantically dug more defensive embankments and constructed a makeshift breastwork using their stone and bison scapula shovels and hoes. After the new defenses proved insufficient to ward off the attackers, the Arikaras retreated into their earth lodges, where they continued to fight for their homes and families. Their fortifications and heroic defense ultimately proved unsuccessful. The three excavated homes at the site reveal the extreme violence of the incident and shed light on northern plains warfare in the late 1700s. Within those three homes, evidence exists that the invaders killed seventy-one men, women, and children and mutilated their bodies. In a ritualistic manner, the invaders scalped their male and female victims, decapitated them, crushed their skulls and faces, removed their hands and feet, and disemboweled them. Then they burned the earth lodges, covering the victims in debris. Scores of other victims may rest within unexcavated lodges, hiding the actual death toll of this violent encounter.

Their cousins to the south, collectively called the Kirikir'is or Kitikiti'sh (Raccoon Eyes People) because of distinctive tattoo designs around their eyes that resembled a raccoon's mask, are sometimes referred to as the Wichitas and Affiliated Tribes or simply the Wichitas (comprising the Kichais, Taovayas, Tawakonis, Yscanis, Wacos, and Wichitas). These nations farmed in the fertile river valleys of the central and southern plains, especially along the tributaries of the Arkansas, Canadian, and Ouachita Rivers. In Texas, they lived in small hamlets and settled villages along the Brazos, Trinity, Sabine, and Red Rivers, where they hunted deer and planted corn, beans, tobacco, sunflowers, and melons. After the acquisition of the horse, some groups supplemented their diet by hunting bison on the plains in the spring and fall, living in mobile tepees made of skins. During the winter, they lived in neat permanent towns with homes consisting of erected cedar posts supporting a large, cone-shaped framework covered with grass or skins. Women built and owned the homes and shelters in their matrilineal societies. Known for their extensive trade networks and their friendliness to strangers and hospitality toward guests, Wichitas traded turquoise pendants, engraved ceramic pottery, and other items with Indigenous merchants, as well as with Spanish, French, and American traders who ventured into the West. Wichitas operated as important intermediaries in the trade between European merchants and the Comanches farther west on the plains.

Around 1400 AD the Wichitas living in the Arkansas River basin experienced increased conflict over resources and territory. In times of trouble, they banded together for defense into larger, fortified towns, usually constructed as sister villages for mutual assistance. Spanish explorer Francisco Vásquez de Coronado encountered Wichitas in Quivira [Kansas] in 1541, finding half a dozen towns, each governed by a chief or headman and subchief who sought suitable sites for villages based on water, trees, grazing, and defensibility. Wichitas participated in the capture and enslavement of women and children, as well as the adoption of such captives acquired from their rivals, like the Pawnees, to bolster their population and replace losses from disease and warfare. Wichita and other Native raiders carried off so many Pawnees that the slave markets at Montreal, New Orleans, and Santa Fe referred to many Indigenous enslaved peoples by the French term *Panis* (anglicized to "Pawnees").

As the Wichitas came under increasing attacks from Spanish and Native adversaries, they constructed strongholds along the Sabine River. For example, the Waco band of the Wichita nation cast up an earthen embankment several feet high at one of their permanent towns near present-day Waco, Texas. Farther south, Tonkawas layered stone breastworks for defense. Other bands used natural defenses by situating their huts in dense briar thickets. Like the Mandans and Hidatsas of the northern plains, the Wichitas dug ditches to deter attackers and deep trenches within fortifications to confuse invaders. Others created subterranean earth lodges where women and children could hide. In one village in open country, the residents dug defensive ditches and heaped the earth into 4-foot-high embankments. At the tops of these walls, they interlaced their tepee poles, forming a breastwork they covered with buffalo hides, through which they cut loopholes to fire their weapons. Some wove brush camouflage shields to screen themselves as they shot at attackers.

By the mid-eighteenth century Wichitas had built fortifications in many of their villages. The chronicler of a Spanish
expedition led by Col. Diego Ortiz Parrilla described one of
these Wichita forts in north-central Texas along the Red River,
built to protect the Wichitas against the Spanish interlopers:
"We clearly discerned a town of tall, oval shaped huts encircled
by a stockade and a ditch. Its entrance road was enclosed in the
same manner and in addition it zig-zagged intricately, with its
gate at the aforementioned river, whose waters flowed by with
a depth of more than a yard and a third."

A few years later Fray Joseph de Calahorra y Sanz described
the same Wichita fort in a letter to the territorial governor:
"In the middle of this settlement is the fortress they built to
resist Colonel don Diego Ortiz Parrilla's campaign. It is made
of split logs, which the Indians have placed separate one from
the other in order to make use of muskets, the weapons they
use, through them." Calahorra y Sanz noted that an earthen
rampart completely surrounded the fortress, as did a deep trench
that prevented approach by horseback. Women and children
who could not defend the village retreated to four subterranean
apartments for refuge. Conditions on the central and southern
plains, like those on the northern plains, required sedentary
people to defend themselves. Like the Mandans and Hidatsas
who lived along the Missouri River, the Arikaras and Wichitas
used the resources available to fortify their communities.

Defensive Sites and Refuge Strongholds

The sections thus far have mainly described the architectural
fortifications of larger, semisedentary nations residing along the
rivers of the Great Plains. Clearly, the time and effort spent in
constructing these large-scale architectural and military earthen
works reflect the importance Native communities placed on
the safety and protection of their inhabitants; self-preservation

is a powerful motivator. In contrast, some simpler defenses could be erected quickly, providing spontaneous short-term safety, and did not require the planning, resources, or labor of the larger village fortifications. Yet even simple construction required time, labor, and resource allocations. A few examples from Montana and Wyoming illustrate these defensive sites and refuge strongholds.

The Alcova Redoubt, on an isolated sandstone butte in central Wyoming, shows how a smaller Indigenous population used architecture to enhance a natural defensive site. Striking features of the location are the three juniper and sandstone walls measuring 732 feet, which intermesh with a sandstone caprock. The east, west, and inner walls were made of vertical juniper poles with woven rock and juniper beams reinforcing sandstone slabs and stacked wood. The east wall is the tallest and longest of the structure. The inner wall served as a secondary defense in case attackers breached the other walls. Eight to twelve bastions large enough for two people provided clear site lines and overlapping areas of projectile fire for defenders armed with bows and arrows, lances, and softball-size river cobblestones (about twenty-six stones were in a pile at each bastion).

The Grapevine Creek battle site on the Crow Indian Reservation in the Bighorn Canyon is another defensive site, constructed by Blackfeet (Piegan) warriors around 1850 on a promontory about 8 miles southwest of present-day Fort Smith, southwest of Hardin, Montana. The Piegan party of thirty-five warriors sought to steal Crow horses in the Bighorn River valley. They followed a Crow party ascending Grapevine Creek southwest toward Hoodoo Creek. A large Crow hunting encampment lay about 5 miles from the battle site. While the Crows butchered a bison, they spied the Piegan raiders. The outnumbered Piegan men knew they could not outrun their enemies, so they ascended a knoll and erected twenty-three

Fig. 8. *A Blackfoot [Blackfeet] Indian on Horseback* by Karl Bodmer. Wikimedia Commons.

U-shaped stone breastworks in a tight cluster to protect them from Crow reprisal for trespassing. Each small breastwork could accommodate one or two men. The Crows did not immediately attack but instead methodically prepared for war through medicine rituals and by adorning appropriate regalia. They alerted the larger encampment nearby to the enemy's presence. Once the battle began, the Crows made several unsuccessful attempts to overrun the Piegan defenses, which the Blackfeet defended from their bastions by throwing rocks and lances and shooting arrows.

The stalemate ended when Crow medicine man Stump Horn arrived. Dressed in a robe with paintings of a bull elk and armed with his weapon ticked with elk horns (his spiritual medicine came from elk), he told the rest of the Crow warriors to rest and watch as he attacked the Blackfeet alone. He zigzagged up the hill like an elk, singing his war song. The Piegan could not hit him with their weapons, which was attributed to his strong medicine. He entered their stronghold and started stabbing them, while the Crow warriors used his diversion to launch another assault up the hill from the south. All but one of the Blackfeet died. The Crows beat the survivor and charged him with returning to his people to tell them what would happen if they tried to enter Crow territory again. Grapevine Creek represents one of the largest intertribal battle locations in the country.

Much smaller sites exist in many locations across the Great Plains. For example, tribes of the northwestern plains, like those of the Blackfeet Confederacy, built refuge strongholds known as war lodges whenever they went on raids. The strongholds' uncomplicated design, ease of construction, and durability matched their overall effectiveness. To conduct a raid, about ten warriors would leave their villages on foot. Men usually formed raiding parties, but childless married couples could also join. When they arrived within one or two days' journey from an enemy camp, they spent several hours erecting a war lodge. The leader of the raid oversaw the construction of the lodge. Where they lacked lumber resources, shelters of rocks or arched willow poles covered with brush sufficed or, as a last resort, warriors might dig a hasty foxhole. Ideally, raiders located their war lodge in a dense thicket or grove of cottonwoods. In such a setting, they built a conical structure of long, heavy pieces of fallen timber to form the framework, which they covered with long pieces of cottonwood bark they procured with sharp knives. They laid heavy fallen cottonwood logs around the outside of the cone several feet high to hold the bark in place and provide ample cover from enemy fire. The timbers also formed an angling doorway that required one to stoop to enter, making it easy to defend the lodge from within.

Once the war lodge was erected, the men spent a few days hunting and drying meat, repairing moccasins, scouting enemy positions, and forming their attack plan. Guarding their war lodge night and day, they took turns at watch duty, with sentries posted at each of the four cardinal directions. After putting on their tokens of good luck, painting their faces, and singing war songs, they commenced the raid. The war lodge provided protection against a surprise preemptive attack and from the elements, especially during winter raids, and also served as a base of operations for scouting, a supply base for the raiders, and an information command center. Plains Crees, Crows, Lakotas, Gros Ventres, Cheyennes, and Assiniboines all built similar war lodge refuge strongholds.

Great Plains tribes experienced and participated in warfare both before and after the arrival of European and American interlopers. Many semisedentary groups like the Mandans and Arikaras constructed substantial forts to defend their villages from raiders and warriors. These fortifications and strongholds took a variety of shapes and sizes. Commonalities existed, however. Whenever possible, leaders chose naturally defensible village sites, often on elevated riverbanks. Indigenous laborers added to the natural defenses by building palisades, bastions, moats, trenches, ditches, and embankments. They used timber, stone, water, and earth in distinct ways to defend their homes. Warriors made shields and protective coverings for their bodies and for their horses. As Europeans arrived, Indigenous peoples faced new challenges of building coalitions and alliances with European and Native neighbors for protection. Indigenous, Spanish, French, British, Canadian, Mexican, and American observers provided descriptions of Native fortifications. Their observations, along with oral histories and the archaeological evidence from many sites, reveal that Indigenous fortifications stretched from the Canadian Prairies to the Texas plains. In addition to the fortified villages constructed by sedentary peoples, warring parties built less sophisticated defenses and war lodge refuges. These diverse types of fortifications provide ample evidence of the widespread existence and intensity of warfare on the Great Plains during the late prehistoric and early historic periods.

CHAPTER TWO

Fur Factories and Trading Posts

In 1763 New Orleans merchant Pierre de Laclède Liguest traveled up the Mississippi River with his wife, Marie-Thérèse Bourgeois Chouteau; their son, Jean-Pierre (Pierre) Chouteau; and his half brother, René-Auguste (Auguste) Chouteau. The following year Laclède dispatched the teenage Auguste, whom he employed as a clerk, and thirty men to build a village on the west bank of the Mississippi just south of the confluence of the Missouri River. They named the community St. Louis, after the reigning French monarch Louis XV. St. Louis eventually grew to become the gateway to the West, and the half brothers Pierre and Auguste and their Chouteau descendants dominated the Missouri River fur trade over the next century.

French Louisiana—the area drained by the Mississippi and its tributaries—encompassed practically all the land east of the Rocky Mountains and west of the Mississippi River. The 828,000-square-mile area stretched from the future Canadian border in the north to the present-day states of Texas and Louisiana in the south. Excluding portions of Texas and the Canadian Prairies, French Louisiana comprised almost the entirety of the Great Plains. When René-Robert Cavelier, sieur de La Salle, traveled down the Mississippi in 1682, he arrived at the river's mouth and claimed the land by right of discovery in the name of the French king Louis XIV and called it Louisiana. The

27

European Doctrine of Discovery justified the way colonial powers laid claim to lands belonging to foreign sovereign nations. This right of discovery could be acquired or forfeited through warfare, exchanged with other nations, or even sold to a third party. Eighty years later, in 1762, when the French realized they were about to lose the French and Indian War, they quietly ceded their right of discovery to their Spanish allies in the secret Treaty of Fontainebleau. They did not want the British, their nemesis, to acquire the vast region. The Spanish thus gained the discovery claims to French Louisiana. The 1763 Treaty of Paris ending the war established the Mississippi River as the boundary between British and Spanish territory.

As the founding citizens of St. Louis, the Chouteaus immediately sought to curry favor with Spanish officials so they could continue to expand their fur-trading enterprise. Auguste sought permission from Spanish governor-general Francisco Luis Héctor de Carondelet to build one of the first fur-trading posts on the eastern borderland of the Great Plains. Carondelet recognized the wisdom of establishing a post to secure peace between the fledgling communities along the west bank of the Mississippi and the Greater and Lesser Osages, powerful nations with a fighting force of 1,250 warriors. Moreover, to ensure Chouteau loyalty to the Spanish crown, Carondelet granted the family a six-year monopoly of the Osage trade in 1794.

Auguste Chouteau named the trading post Fort Carondelet to win the governor's approval. Carondelet issued guidelines for the fort's construction. He recommended that a strong stockade of logs 6 inches thick and 16 feet tall (12 feet above the ground) surround the entire complex. The palisaded fort would have four bastions two stories tall that ensured clear sight and firing lines along every wall. The bastions' second story would include loopholes cut in the plank work from which to defend the post. Four cannons and four swivel guns would reinforce the defenses. A solid plank door 6.5 feet high and 5 feet wide, mounted on hinges with bolts and a lock of iron, would secure the entryway. Carondelet wanted brick walls for the 10-foot-tall first story; the second floor would consist of 10-inch-square planks laid horizontally to the height of 9 feet. Planks 2 to 3 inches thick would form the floors. Materials for the pitched roof would include a combination of slate, timber, and turf.

Carondelet's plan called for the trading post to form an exact square 32 by 32 feet, consisting of several parts: fortified barracks to house a small Spanish garrison of twenty soldiers, separate lodging for the commandant, a powder magazine of brick and stone, a kitchen and privies (bathrooms), and a large warehouse to conduct the trade of furs and skins. Evidence suggests that to save time and money, the Chouteaus did not build the fort to Carondelet's specifications. Nevertheless, after Governor Carondelet approved their application, the Chouteaus constructed the fur-trading post in 1795 on Halley's Bluff, high ground overlooking the Osage villages near the Osage River, several dozen miles east of the present-day Missouri-Kansas border.

Pierre and his sons Auguste Pierre and Pierre Chouteau Jr. operated the post, forging a friendship with the Osages through gift-giving, kinship ties, and trade. Both the Chouteaus and the Osages benefited from the growing exchange of goods: the Osages gained access to manufactured products, becoming more affluent than their Indigenous neighbors, and the Chouteaus profited from the resulting business at the post. Moreover, French, Spanish, and American settlers along the Missouri slept a little sounder at night knowing they were safe.

Fort Carondelet represents one of the forts built on the Great Plains to facilitate the fur trade. In this chapter, we examine the general conditions of the fur factories and forts of the Great Plains. We analyze the entry of the United States into the international competition for furs and the role of forts in public and private interests. Individuals, partners, and the government constructed factories and forts. The Missouri Fur Company and its successors built many of the earliest fur posts on the plains, but soon the American Fur Company ushered in a new wave of fort construction and competition. Fort Union's chief factor Kenneth McKenzie used cutthroat competition to force entrepreneurs William Sublette and Robert Campbell to sell their Missouri River forts and business interests to him after they challenged the AFC's hegemony on the Upper Missouri. As beaver numbers declined through overtrapping, and silk hats increased in popularity, plains posts such as Fort Benton, Fort Union, Fort Laramie, and Bent's Fort transitioned to trading with Native hunters for bison robes.

Conditions of the Fur Factories and Forts

During the first half of the nineteenth century, fort building on the Great Plains by non-Indigenous nations commenced. The government and private companies built factories and trading posts to expand or defend land claims or for commercial trade purposes, or both. Some outposts served frontier settlements as defensive structures and as staging and supply depots to launch American exploration or expansion expeditions; others operated as commercial centers promoting trade between Indigenous, European, and American trappers and merchants. Fur factories functioned as trade centers in times of peace and as frontier fortifications during periods of animosity.

Because the architecture of trading posts resembled military fortifications, contemporaries used the terms *fur post* and *fort* interchangeably. As with the plans for Fort Carondelet, square or rectangular palisades enclosed most forts, protecting the traders and their valuable goods from potentially hostile customers. Vertical timbers buried in a trench and extending 12 to 18 feet upward to a sharpened point, modeled after the fortified

Indigenous villages along the Missouri (see chapter 1), provided a distinctive look. Two square blockhouses or bastions set at opposing corners of the palisade provided clear sight lines and overlapping cover. Often two stories, the bastions usually had small cannons and loopholes through which defenders could fire their rifles at intruders attempting to scale the walls. Fur companies built the roofs of the interior buildings 4 or 5 feet below the tops of the pickets to allow sentries to walk on top of, and fire from, defensible positions.

The posts were in an inhospitable environment, and the buildings within provided few of the comforts of eastern cities. A central open courtyard featured a flagpole and often a cannon. In smaller forts, the rooms connected the outside walls, saving space and lumber. Larger forts often had stables or storage buildings along the outer walls. Roofs consisted of rough-hewn lumber covered with dirt or sod. The chief factor or bourgeois (manager) lived on the upper floor or in a separate mansion, usually the most opulent structure in the fort, located opposite the main gate for visual effect. A dining hall and business office inside the main house and a kitchen outside provided comfort and served the trade purposes of the post. The largest posts sometimes had a powder magazine made of stone or brick, employee barracks, a blacksmith shop, and an icehouse.

Fur posts on the Canadian Prairies (see chapter 5) differed from their southern cousins. *Poteaux en terre* (posts in earth) structures had walls made from timbers placed vertically into trenches. In contrast, Canadian *poteaux sur sole* (posts on sill) construction placed posts vertically on wood or stone sills to prevent wood rot. A third French Métis construction method, known as Red River frame, or *pièce sur pièce* (timber on timber), used grooved, vertical logs raised on a wooden sill. Horizontal logs with tenons slipped into the vertical grooves formed the interior wall, which was plastered and whitewashed. In all three types of construction, workers packed grass and mud (*bouzillées*) or stone and plaster mortar (*pierrottées*) between the posts for privacy and to make the structure wind and weather resistant.

In addition to the palisaded forts, some Great Plains forts used adobe in their construction, reflecting southwestern Indigenous and Hispanic influences. Adobe worked well in the dry climate on the high plains where few trees grew. After the American Fur Company purchased Fort William, the company covered the fort with adobe and renamed it Fort John on the Laramie (known as Fort Laramie after the U.S. government purchased it in 1849). Adobe insulated against summer heat and winter cold and allowed for unique structure shapes. Notably, Bent's Fort used adobe to create circular bastions and other curved features.

Great Plains trading posts reflected an economy of scale. Four of the largest posts included Bent's Fort on the Arkansas, Fort Laramie on the Platte, Fort Union on the Missouri, and Fort Garry near the confluence of the Assiniboine and Red River of the North on the Canadian Prairies. Subsidiary trading posts and wintering posts operated year-round but were smaller and simpler. The smallest wintering houses did not have fortifications and usually consisted simply of a crude cabin or dugout used for a few trading seasons.

Private fur trade entrepreneurs built many of the early American forts on the plains to foster the growth of the trade in beaver pelts, deer hides, and bison robes with Indigenous trappers and hunters; compete against rival fur companies; and capitalize on other mercantile endeavors, such as travel on the Santa Fe Trail. Like the Indigenous defenses described in chapter 1, the fur-trading posts were constructed at strategic locations along streams and rivers or in neutral zones where traditional enemies might encamp near one another peacefully. Fur traders constructed posts along the Arkansas, Missouri,

Platte, Rio Grande, Yellowstone, and Saskatchewan Rivers and along the great fur trade routes that eventually became the overland trails. These posts provided warehouses for furs and hides and equipped boats and caravans with needed supplies to conduct trade farther upriver or where the Great Plains met the Rocky Mountains on the western borderland. The sutlers and traders at the forts encouraged peace, which was good for business. Nevertheless, fur-trading posts needed to be prepared against Indigenous attacks designed to steal property, "collect rent," or simply destroy the post to defend tribal sovereignty or prevent enemy neighbors from benefiting from the trade.

Early Fur-Trading Posts and Factories

In 1796 the U.S. Congress passed the Intercourse Act, which permitted the government to establish a series of "factories" or governmentally licensed and operated fur-trading posts in the West. In these forts, Indigenous people could trade hides, pelts, furs, and other objects for manufactured goods such as blankets, kettles, firearms, and powder. The purpose of these factories was to establish peace and friendship between the United States and Native nations. Government-run factory systems operated over the next twenty-five years in trading houses on Native ground.

In 1800 several events transpired that changed the history of the Great Plains. The Spanish retroceded the Louisiana Territory back to Napoleonic France in the secret Treaty of San Ildefonso. Meanwhile, Spanish governor-general Juan Manuel de Salcedo replaced Carondelet and ended the Chouteau monopoly, granting trading rights instead to one of the family's rivals, the fiery Spaniard Manuel de Lisa. In 1802 Pierre Chouteau sold the fort to Lisa, who withdrew the garrison and abandoned the post. American explorer Zebulon Pike passed by the remnants of Fort Carondelet on August 17, 1806, just a decade after its

Fig. 9. Fort Mandan. Wikimedia Commons.

construction, and noted that the buildings were in disrepair and overgrown with vegetation. His description provides additional evidence that Chouteau had not built the fort to the grandiose standards Carondelet had recommended and partially funded.

In 1803 the Doctrine of Discovery rights to Louisiana transferred from French to American possession. The third president of the United States, Thomas Jefferson, sent diplomats to France to negotiate free trade on the Mississippi River, hoping to purchase the right to warehouse trade goods in New Orleans. Jefferson's diplomats were thrilled when Napoleon's aide offered to sell the entire Louisiana Territory to the United States for $15 million. For this sum, the United States acquired the right of discovery of the Mississippi River drainage—828,000 square miles—which carried with it the notion that only the United States would be authorized to interact with the Native nations who still possessed their right of occupancy.

Jefferson appointed his private secretary, Meriwether Lewis, to command an expedition to the Pacific Northwest via the Missouri and Columbia Rivers, seeking to initiate an American presence in the recently acquired Louisiana Territory. Jefferson tasked the expedition with the goal of finding a commercial water route to the Pacific Ocean to accelerate the American fur trade with the Chinese. Lewis chose a talented fellow Virginian, William Clark, to accompany him. Their completion of a transcontinental route across the Great Plains and their presence in what became jointly occupied Oregon Territory set in motion America's process of becoming a continental nation.

Along the way, William Clark oversaw the construction of the first American fort on the Great Plains along the Missouri River near the Knife River villages of the Mandans and Hidatsas in modern North Dakota. Construction continued from November 2 to 27, 1804. Meriwether Lewis recorded in his journal on November 2 that he named the post Fort Mandan "in honour of our Neighbours," whom they found friendly and hospitable. Sgt. Patrick Gass of the Lewis and Clark Expedition described the fort as follows: "The huts were in two rows, containing four rooms each, and joined at one end forming an angle. When raised about seven feet high a floor of puncheons or split plank were laid, and covered with grass and clay, which made a warm loft. The upper part projected a foot over and the roofs were made shed-fashion, rising from the inner side, and making the outer wall about 18 feet high. The part not enclosed by the huts we intend to picket. In the angle formed by the two rows of huts we built two rooms, for holding our provisions and stores." Northwest trader Francois-Antoine Larocque, who visited Fort Mandan on December 16, 1804, noted, "The whole is made so strong as to be almost cannon ball proof. The two ranges of houses do not join one another but are joined by a piece of fortification made in the form of a semi-circle that can defend two sides of the Fort, on the top of which they keep sentry all night. A sentinel is likewise kept all day walking in the Fort." Throughout the winter, Lewis and Clark traded with the Mandans and Hidatsas in much the same way as future fur posts did, although with a more limited inventory.

An Arikara named Too Né (Eagle Feather) assisted Lewis and Clark as a guide and diplomat. While in St. Louis in 1805, Too Né drew a map of his country, indicating the Indigenous homelands full of people living in sovereign, fortified towns. His map, which he delivered with the declaration "Here is my country," delineated the courses of the rivers as well as friendly and enemy neighbors, village locations, and Native place names. Significantly, not only did he include the fortified Indigenous villages of the Upper Missouri, but he also drew a North West Company fur post, Fort Assiniboine, which he labeled "Fort N. Ouest Companie." Unfortunately, Too Né died from disease before he could return home from his visit to President Jefferson in Washington DC, sparking decades of Arikara animosity toward American traders.

After William Clark returned from the expedition in September 1806, he received a government appointment as Indian agent for tribes in Missouri and the Great Plains and was tasked with constructing the first government-run trading post on the plains. In the fall of 1808 militia brigadier general Clark and his party of eighty men traveled overland to Fire Prairie, on the south bank of the Missouri near present-day Sibley, Missouri. Arriving in September, Clark ordered the men to begin construction of Fort Osage (originally named Fort Clark) on the bluff, 100 feet above the river and 300 miles above the confluence of the Missouri and Mississippi. The next day, he sent Capt. Nathan Boone and an interpreter, Paul Loisel, to summon the Osages to the fort. Meanwhile, six keelboats under the command of Capt. Eli B. Clemson delivered eighty-one men and goods from Fort Bellefontaine to help build and supply the fort. Reuben Lewis, Meriwether Lewis's brother, served as Osage subagent.

Like Chouteau's Fort Carondelet, this hybrid of factory and fort promoted peace and friendship with the Great and Little Osage Nations through trade. In addition to forming an alliance

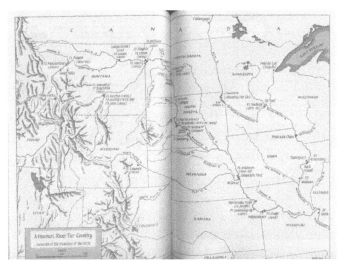

Fig. 10. *Missouri River Fur Country* map. From David Lavender, *The Fist in the Wilderness* (Lincoln: University of Nebraska Press, 1998), 227.

with the United States, the factory encouraged Osage commercial consumerism. After encumbering influential tribal leaders with consumer debt over time, the government could forgive those debts in exchange for land cessions. The U.S. government appointed Pierre Chouteau as Osage Indian agent. He negotiated the Treaty of Fort Clark, wherein the Osages ceded much of eastern Missouri to the United States. Rather than subjugation and Native dispossession by expensive military force, fostering dependency and indebtedness through trade proved less violent and less expensive—American conquest on the cheap.

Osage leaders like Chiefs White Hair and Walking Rain benefited as well, as their influence and prestige grew by providing access to material goods for their people, acquiring powder and ball to fight their enemies, and forming peaceful alliances with the United States. In addition, they received use of the blacksmith, a mill, plows, houses for the main chiefs, and the government trading factory and retained the right to hunt on any of the ceded land. Goods included rifles, powder, lead, tobacco, knives, paint, blankets, and sundry items. Osages viewed American traders and merchants as guests carrying on the fur trade within Osage territory.

The Missouri Fur Company's Fort-Building Ventures

After reports of Lewis and Clark's discoveries started to circulate, private entrepreneurs began fur-trading operations beyond the confines of the factory system. Spanish entrepreneur Manuel de Lisa, backed by the powerful Chouteaus, organized an expedition and ascended the Missouri in 1807, establishing Fort Raymond (a.k.a. Fort Remon or Fort Lisa) at the confluence of the Bighorn and Yellowstone Rivers in south-central Montana. This was one of the first American fur posts on the Great Plains, and he achieved moderate success trading with the Crows, a resident tribe that trapped beaver. In March 1809 Lisa invited prominent citizens to join him in organizing the St. Louis Missouri Fur Company. St. Louis served as a western gateway and as an outfitting center for expeditions traveling to the Upper Missouri, the central plains and, after Mexican independence in 1821, Santa Fe. Lisa's company had the backing of the powerful St. Louis elite: Pierre and Auguste Chouteau, Andrew Henry, Gov. Meriwether Lewis's brother Reuben, and Gen. William Clark all served on the company's board of directors. Clark believed that private American fur traders could trade with Indians and trap for furs if they operated at least 300 miles beyond the reach of the nearest government factory. With the energetic leadership of Lisa, and with Andrew Henry and French-Canadian Pierre Menard as field captains, St. Louis newspaper editor Joseph Charless concluded that the company had "every prospect of becoming a force of incalculable advantage, not only to the individuals engaged in the enterprise, but the community at large."

The company's grand plans included erecting various trading posts among Upper Missouri tribes and garnering the trade of the entire region, drawing it away from British, French, and Spanish traders. As the fur trade was a river-dependent industry, the primary objective of the Missouri Fur Company (MFC) included trading near the headwaters of the Missouri, hundreds of miles beyond the reach of the government trading houses. Clark desired to secure for America the fur trade then flowing into Britain's hands via the North West Company and Hudson's Bay Company and to win for America the Upper Missouri tribes' loyalty. He envisioned the fur company as the means to accomplish both ends. The MFC constructed several additional trading posts: another Fort Lisa, 37 miles above the Platte, for trade with the Omahas, Otos-Missourias, Iowas, and Pawnees; Cedar Island post for the Lakotas and Yanktons; one for the Mandan and Hidatsa villages at Knife River; and another at the Three Forks for the Crows and Blackfeet.

Clark's extensive involvement in the MFC ensured that the trading houses operated smoothly. He arranged for boatloads of provisions to travel upstream to supply the forts while other partners remained in the field. Clark's commingling of government and personal business appeared suspect to St. Louisans, though his personal ventures occurred in regions beyond the reach of the government factories. The MFC achieved success among the Omahas, Poncas, Otos, and Ioways, nations closer to St. Louis. Fort Lisa became the most important trading post in present-day Nebraska. Lisa married an Omaha wife and raised a family, cementing kinship relations with the tribe.

In contrast, setbacks plagued the MFC's efforts on the Missouri River above the confluence of the Platte, the dividing line between the Upper and Lower Missouri. A few Indigenous nations opposed the Upper Missouri fur trade. American trappers became entangled in the rivalry between the Mandans, Lakotas, and Arikaras. When a large party of Americans and their Mandan and Lakota partners tried to escort Mandan chief Sheheke-shote and his wife, Yellow Corn, through Arikara territory, they met with hostility. In the violence that followed, Arikara warriors killed four trappers, wounded a dozen more, and stole half the provisions intended to resupply the MFC forts.

Other challenges plagued the MFC on the Upper Missouri. MFC men built a fort as far to the northwest as the Three Forks of the Missouri, on the western fringe of the Great Plains. The trappers' returns on beaver pelts exceeded expectations, but so did the resistance they faced from the Blackfeet. The Atsinas, part of the Blackfeet Confederacy, repeatedly attacked trapping parties. They killed a dozen men, including John Potts and George Drouillard, who had earlier accompanied the Lewis and Clark Expedition. Atsinas raided an MFC cache of goods and furs on the Yellowstone. The MFC Cedar Island post, above the Missouri's Grand Detour, inexplicably burned down, destroying $12,000–$15,000 worth of furs and goods. Business competition arrived in 1811 when Wilson Price Hunt, agent of John Jacob Astor's American Fur Company, led a party of Astorians up the Missouri River. Moreover, an economic depression in Europe kept fur prices low, limiting profit. These challenges collectively forced the MFC to dissolve and restructure in 1812.

A New Era of Fort Building

Following the War of 1812, laissez-faire economic practices and the germination of a market economy took root in America. Fur traders and companies resented the government-sponsored factories and governmental regulation of the fur trade. They found a champion for their cause in Missouri senator Thomas Hart Benton. Benton contended that the factories had outlived their usefulness and were far too expensive to maintain. Instead, he proposed free enterprise with American traders complying with regulations as the norm. Swayed by Benton's argument, Congress pulled the plug on the government factory system in 1822, and Fort Osage began a new era as a supplier for the Santa Fe Trail. Government interests shifted to the construction of military forts such as Atkinson and Leavenworth (see chapter 4).

With the privatization of government-run factories like Fort Osage, entrepreneurs and fur companies began vying for the Missouri River and overland trails trade. After Manuel Lisa died in August 1820, the MFC was rechartered under Joshua Pilcher's leadership, ushering in a new era of fort building. Pilcher traveled up the Missouri in the spring of 1822 and rebuilt an MFC post to trade with the Mandans and Hidatsas at the Knife River villages. The MFC rebuilt Cedar Fort at White River and Fort Raymond at the mouth of the Bighorn River.

Restructuring the company did not eliminate challenges for the MFC and other traders and trappers. Arikaras tried to stop Pilcher from descending the Missouri in the fall of 1822. They assaulted one of his clerks that winter. In the spring of 1823 a group of Arikaras fought against William H. Ashley and Andrew Henry's upstart fur company, the future Rocky Mountain Fur Company, as they ascended the Missouri with the intent to trap beavers as mountaineers or mountain men. The Arikaras did not want to relinquish their profitable role as fur trade intermediaries or have Americans doing the trapping, and the level of violence escalated. On June 2, 1823, several hundred Arikaras attacked Ashley, Henry, and their men near the confluence of the Grand and Missouri. Arikaras killed fifteen and wounded twelve others in one of the worst fur trade disasters on the plains. Ashley dared not attack the Arikaras' fortified villages, so he retreated downriver and sent word and the wounded to Fort Atkinson, calling for military reinforcements. Col. Henry Leavenworth headed upstream on June 18 with two cannons, 230 U.S. soldiers, seven hundred Lakota allies, and fifty trappers to punish the Arikaras.

What followed was the first major U.S. military battle with a Great Plains Indian nation. Lakota allies rode ahead and started the fight early, killing a dozen Arikaras. On August 9 Leavenworth arrived. Viewing the Arikaras fortified inside their palisaded village, the colonel recognized the futility of a direct assault. Instead, troops bombarded the village, killing Chief Grey Eyes, one of the principal American antagonists, but having negligible effect on the Arikara defenses. After several days of the siege, the Arikaras sued for peace. But disagreements between Leavenworth, who wanted peace, and fur company officials, who wanted revenge and restitution, led to the rejection of the cease-fire offer. In response, the Arikaras fled their fortifications during the night of August 14, and the American troops withdrew downstream, with Pilcher's men burning the Arikara villages as punishment for attacking the fur traders. Unsurprisingly, hostilities continued between the Arikaras and American traders on the Upper Missouri. The Arikaras blockaded the Upper Missouri and forced Ashley and Henry to abandon their fort-building campaign. Instead, they eliminated the need for trading posts by holding annual summer rendezvous in the Rocky Mountain territory of the Shoshones along the Green, Bear, and Snake Rivers over the next fifteen years, largely negating the need to build costly forts along the rivers between 1825 and 1835. After the smallpox epidemic of 1837, the Arikaras' blockade ended when they moved north to the Knife River villages near Fort Clark.

Meanwhile, the Columbia Fur Company (CFC) began to construct forts on the Missouri River in 1822. Consisting of former employees of the Hudson's Bay and North West Companies who found themselves unemployed after those companies merged in 1821 (discussed in chapter 5), the C F C formed in St. Louis, and its employees transported goods overland from its bases on the Mississippi to the Missouri. William Clark, now superintendent of Indian affairs at St. Louis, granted the C F C a license to trade with the Dakotas on the Minnesota River and with the Mandans, Hidatsas, and Crows on the Missouri. The C F C constructed its flagship post, Fort Tecumseh, at the confluence of the Teton (Bad) and Missouri Rivers in central South Dakota. C F C employees built a handful of other forts, including Fort Floyd in present-day North Dakota, to facilitate trade on the Upper Missouri. In 1827 Astor's American Fur Company bought out the C F C to form a western department, known as the Upper Missouri Outfit, with Pierre Chouteau Jr. as the chief executive.

Employee James Kipp constructed an Upper Missouri Outfit post just south of the Mandan village Mih-Tutta-Hang-Kusch in 1830 and christened it the Fort Clark Trading Post. In 1832 the steamboat *Yellowstone* arrived, the first to successfully navigate the Missouri River to North Dakota, carrying fifteen hundred gallons of alcohol as well as other trade goods and supplies. The *Yellowstone* returned to St. Louis with one hundred packs of beaver pelts and numerous bison robes. Artist George Catlin visited Fort Clark in 1832, and artist Karl Bodmer and explorer Prince Maximilian of Wied-Neuwied stayed there during the winter of 1833–34. These artists provided the earliest visual representations of the rectangular fort, which measured 120 by 160 feet and included a palisade. Inside the fort, head trader Francis A. Chardon lived in the bourgeois house. Between 1834 and 1839 Chardon kept a journal of his life at Fort Clark, chronicling the highs and lows of the post's history.

One of those low points occurred when the steamboat *St. Peters* docked at Fort Clark on June 19, 1837. Although company officials quarantined the vessel because of a smallpox outbreak,

Fig. 11. *Mih-Tutta-Hang-Kusch, Mandan Village* on the Missouri, with Fort Clark depicted, by Karl Bodmer, 1834. Wikimedia Commons.

the infection unfortunately spread when Natives sneaked onto the boat, sparking the 1837 smallpox epidemic on the Upper Missouri. Chardon documented the horrific pandemic in his journal, describing the ordeal that wiped out 90 percent of the Mandan inhabitants of Mih-Tutta-Hang-Kusch. The survivors abandoned the village and joined the Hidatsas near the mouth of the Knife River. About half of the Arikaras survived the epidemic, and in 1838 they moved upriver into the abandoned Mandan village adjacent to Fort Clark. A few years after suffering a second smallpox outbreak in 1856, the Arikaras moved upstream again in 1862 to Like-a-Fishhook Village (near Fort Berthold trading post) to join the Mandans and Hidatsas, thus forming the Three Affiliated Tribes.

American Fur Company Outposts

By the early 1830s the competition between fur companies on the Upper Missouri River began to take its toll on most

Fig. 12. *Fort Union on the Missouri*, by Karl Bodmer. Wikimedia Commons.

upstart companies. Those that survived competed against the American Fur Company (AFC), which grew in significance after establishing its Upper Missouri Outfit. Founded in 1828, the AFC constructed its flagship outpost, Fort Union, near the confluence of the Missouri and Yellowstone Rivers, a location recommended by Lewis and Clark twenty-three years earlier. Fort Union functioned as the administrative center for the Upper Missouri Outfit and its proprietors, William Laidlaw, Daniel Lamont, and Kenneth McKenzie. Seven nations— Assiniboine, Plains Cree, Blackfeet, Plains Chippewa, Mandan, Hidatsa, and Arikara—exchanged bison robes and other furs here for goods from around the world. In its favorable location on the western edge of present-day North Dakota, Fort Union served as the major collection and distribution center for the northern plains fur trade from 1828 to 1867, becoming one of the grandest fur trade posts in the United States.

The AFC built additional forts extending the fur trade into Blackfeet territory. In 1833 Alexander Culbertson signed a three-year contract to clerk for the Upper Missouri Outfit. After arriving at Fort Union, he received his assignment to Fort McKenzie in present-day Montana. As a trader at one of the principal AFC forts in Blackfeet territory, he married a Piegan woman three weeks after his arrival to cement ties with the Blackfeet Confederacy. Historians are unsure how long his marriage lasted, but the company promoted the talented employee to bourgeois of the fort in 1834. Returning to Fort Union as chief trader in 1840, he married the teenage Natawista Iksina, a Kainai (Blood) Blackfoot, and they had five children together. Her diplomacy and skill extended his success at Fort Union and secured his promotion to superintendent of the Upper Missouri Outfit, overseeing all company forts on the Missouri and Yellowstone Rivers until 1847. That year he established Fort Benton (see chapters 3 and 5), a successful fur-trading post and the farthest a steamboat could travel up the Missouri before encountering the impassable Great Falls.

Challenge to the Monopoly

Under Culbertson's leadership and in the years that followed, Fort Union became one of the most profitable fur-trading posts. It experienced an annual exchange of twenty-five thousand buffalo robes and $100,000 in merchandise until the U.S. military purchased it in 1867. Fort Union's success bred jealousy among its rivals, including Robert Campbell and William Sublette, who had been suppliers to the Rocky Mountain Rendezvous in the early 1830s. Although the rendezvous system worked well for the beaver pelt trade, transporting bulky and heavy buffalo robes meant erecting forts for Native hunters to trade at, and with steamboats to transport the hides downriver. With their

Fig. 13. Robert Campbell. By permission of Andy Hahn, executive director, Campbell House Museum.

profits from the rendezvous, Campbell and Sublette sought to challenge the A F C by building Fort William near Fort Union and another dozen rival Missouri River posts adjacent to A F C ones. Campbell arrived at the confluence of the Yellowstone and Missouri Rivers near Fort Union on August 28 with furs and proceeds from the 1833 rendezvous. Meanwhile, Sublette boarded the steamboat *Otto* and, with a large keelboat full of merchandise, supplies, equipment, liquor, and thirty men, set out for the Upper Missouri, establishing posts at strategic points to trade with the Lakotas and other nations.

In September 1833 Campbell took responsibility for building Fort William, named in Sublette's honor, while Sublette and nine or ten men floated the summer's furs down the Missouri to St. Louis. Construction on the fort, 2 miles by land or 6 miles by water below Fort Union, proceeded rapidly. Writing to his mother before Sublette left, Campbell reported that he and his sixty men had completed four houses in ten days. He expected to stay at the fort all winter, trading with the Crees and Assiniboines for beaver skins and bison robes. The lucrative trade proved too tempting to resist, despite the hazards and discomforts of life in and around the forts. In a letter to his sister Anne, Campbell explained that his reason for staying in the fur trade was not the excitement or love of adventure but "to make money." "Were it not this," he lamented, "we would all endeavor to fashion ourselves to civilized life and no doubt feel ten times the happiness which we enjoy here."

In building their main operation post, Campbell deftly organized the men and directed the fort's construction. Fort William was 150 by 130 feet, with a stockade of 18-foot cottonwood pickets. The boss's house was a double cabin that stood back, opposite the front door, and consisted of two 18-by-20-foot rooms with a 12-foot-wide passage between them. The post contained a store and warehouse 40 feet long and 18 feet wide, a carpenter's shop, blacksmith's shop, icehouse, meat house, and two splendid bastions. By November 15 only a few buildings remained unfinished, so Campbell sent most of his men out to find Arapahos, Cheyennes, Crows, Sioux, and other tribes to alert them of the new fort and invite them to come and trade. Shortly thereafter, a large village of Assiniboines assembled near the fort.

Campbell's Fort William journal demonstrates that many successful fur trade entrepreneurs were serious-minded, sober, religious, and did not fit the devil-may-care mountaineer stereotype. Campbell let his men take Sundays off and devoted time to reading the Bible, writing letters to family and friends, and fasting. He expressed gratitude to God "for his gracious goodness in preserving me through all the dangers I have passed." He prayed for wisdom, understanding, and judgment "to lead well and incline his heart to seek after thee as the one thing needful without which all worldly gain is but dross."

Campbell found loving his neighbor quite difficult, however, especially when the resourceful McKenzie, who managed Fort Union, responded to his competitor with threats and cutthroat tactics. With over five hundred men employed and thousands of dollars' worth of trade goods concentrated in one of the grandest forts of the Upper Missouri, McKenzie felt confident that he could thwart Campbell and Sublette's operations. McKenzie gave his agents permission to pay any price to secure the Indigenous people's furs, driving prices out of the reach of Fort William's representatives. He sent spies to report on the activities at Fort William and used homemade liquor from his still to secure Native customers. McKenzie even stole Campbell's favorite dog. McKenzie's costly methods wiped out AFC profits but enabled his agents to outbid Campbell on all parts of the river. By spring Campbell had only 100 packs of buffalo robes (10 robes to the pack), while McKenzie had 430 packs.

McKenzie used similar tactics all along the Missouri River to ruin Campbell and Sublette. AFC officials met with Sublette in New York in January and February 1834 for a week's worth of negotiations that resulted in their purchasing Campbell and Sublette's river posts and merchandise, thus buying out the competition.

Decline of Beavers and Rise of Bison

Dwindling profits and increased competition at the last few rendezvous in 1832–34 indicated to Campbell and Sublette that the beaver trade was fading as beaver numbers declined. While Ashley's rendezvous system had been revolutionary, effective when mountain men trapped beavers, Campbell and Sublette saw the wisdom in returning to the old, established method of building trading posts where Indigenous hunters brought buffalo robes to trade. They correctly anticipated that the post trader would replace the mountain man and rendezvous system during the next surge in economic activity—the trading of tanned bison robes. Following the 1833 rendezvous and after the sale of their river forts to the AFC, Campbell and Sublette made plans to construct a central trading post to control the vast interior bison robe trade. The establishment of a post partway between St. Louis and the hunting grounds meant traders would have a shorter distance for transporting their supplies and hides to and from the mountains. Not only would the shorter trip be less hazardous, but if constructed in the right location, the fort could operate year-round. Additionally, because Campbell and Sublette's financial success depended on Native hunters, the partners agreed that a second Fort William (later renamed Fort Laramie) should be in the heart of bison country.

In 1834 Campbell and Sublette selected a site near the confluence of the Laramie and North Platte Rivers about 800 miles from St. Louis and around thirty days' march from Independence, Missouri. It was strategically located at the intersection of the Great Platte route to the Rockies and a trappers' trail that connected Fort Pierre in present-day South Dakota with fur-trading centers in Colorado, Taos, and Santa Fe, and it was a convenient place for the Arapahos, Cheyennes, and Lakotas to exchange buffalo robes for manufactured goods. Campbell and Sublette used the profits from the sale of their Missouri River posts and supplies to the AFC to finance the construction. About three-quarters of a mile up the Laramie River from its junction with the Platte, Sublette crossed over to the west bank and dispatched a dozen men with provisions to begin building the fort that summer. The partners' new Fort William on the Laramie became an oasis in the desert that served as a storage facility for the bulky bison robes and offered protection from the elements, raiding parties, and rival companies. Recognizing its value, officials from the AFC soon made an offer to buy this Fort William (renamed Fort John and, after 1849, Fort Laramie) as well, which Campbell and Sublette accepted. In less than a year the American Fur Company had gained control of both Fort Williams, but Campbell and Sublette had made a substantial profit from their business dealings and had constructed a fort that became perhaps the most important to emigrant travel in the 1840s and 1850s (see chapter 3) and to military endeavors in the 1850s–70s (see chapter 5).

The qualities of leadership and enterprise that brought Campbell success in making money in the fur trade carried over into his St. Louis business affairs after his return to civilization, and he became one of the city's leading citizens and wealthiest merchants. Supplying western forts from his mercantile store in St. Louis, Campbell continued to participate and prosper in the fur trade. For example, he provided the financial backing for Alexander Harvey and Charles Primeau in the late 1840s and 1850s to continue to challenge the AFC on the Upper Missouri by building Fort Campbell directly across the river from Fort Benton. Fort Campbell did a surprisingly good business in bison robes, amounting to about half that of Fort Benton, an AFC post with strong connections to Blackfeet hunters.

The Importance of Bent's Fort

Matching the importance of Fort Union and Fort Laramie on the Upper Missouri and Platt Rivers, Bent's Fort became the center of the Arkansas River trade and an important stop on the Santa Fe Trail. Recognizing the opportunity to profit from the fur trade, in 1831 William Bent and Ceran St. Vrain formed Bent, St. Vrain & Company, a fur business that gained importance on the southern plains. They soon constructed a stockade near Pueblo on the north side of the Arkansas River, which served as an outpost to facilitate trade with Native hunters for beaver pelts and bison robes.

Southern Cheyenne warrior Yellow Wolf informed William Bent that if the company constructed a fort farther downstream, it would be better located to trade with the southern Cheyennes and Arapahos for bison robes. In 1833 the partners constructed an adobe Bent's Fort on the north side of the Arkansas River, about a dozen miles above the mouth of the Purgatoire near what is now La Junta, Colorado. The adobe fort quickly became a commercial trading center and the headquarters of the Bent, St. Vrain & Company's expanding trade empire. In 1837 the company expanded its enterprise to include Fort St. Vrain to the north, and in 1845 it added Fort Adobe to the south, with company stores constructed in New Mexico at Taos and Santa Fe. From 1833 to 1849 Bent's Fort was a stopping point along the mountain route of the Santa Fe Trail (see chapter 3). Just as Clark's Fort Osage had facilitated trade with the Osages, Kansas, Otos, and Missourias, Bent's Fort served as a trade center for southern plains tribes including the Southern Cheyenne and Arapaho Nations, as well as a convenient rendezvous point for trappers, mountain men, and explorers.

Private fur trade entrepreneurs built early American forts on the plains to foster the growth of the pelt and robe trade with tribes, compete against rival fur companies, or capitalize on other mercantile endeavors such as the Santa Fe trade route. Other posts operated as commercial trading houses for trappers, traders, and overland emigration. Still others housed soldiers policing the overland trails. Fort construction was concentrated along the Arkansas, Missouri, Platte, Rio Grande, and Yellowstone Rivers and along the overland trails. Fort building on the Great Plains initially focused on trading posts to secure beaver pelts and bison robes from the Lewis and Clark era until the 1840s. As the fur trade declined, companies simply abandoned most fur posts. The federal government purchased a few of them, however, and rebuilt, repurposed, and expanded them as way stations for overland emigration, which increased along the Oregon, California, Mormon, and Santa Fe Trails.

CHAPTER THREE

Overland Trail Emporiums

On October 8, 1856, the Martin Handcart Company, a group of
several hundred Latter-Day Saint pioneers pulling their meager
supplies in handcarts toward the Salt Lake Valley, arrived at
Fort Laramie. They expected to be restocked at the fort by supplies sent from the valley but were disappointed to find that no
goods awaited them. The company, having left in August and
traveling late in the season, had survived on dwindling rations.
And winter storms threatened to halt travel on Wyoming's high
plains west of the fort. Few members of the group had money
with which to buy any of the goods sold at the fort.

In need of recruits, army officials at Fort Laramie pointed
out to the young men traveling in the handcart company the
cozy adobe and log rooms used by the soldiers stationed at the
fort. These recruiters contrasted the ample meals that the soldiers enjoyed with the meager rations available to the pioneers.
Their persuasive words resonated with nineteen-year-old Aaron
Harrison, who reflected on the conditions at Fort Laramie
throughout the day as he helped pull his family's handcart for
17 miles through increasingly rocky terrain. That evening Aaron
informed his parents and siblings that he intended to return to
Fort Laramie and enlist in the army. Despite his mother's pleas,
Aaron and three other young men from the Martin Company
walked back to Fort Laramie and enlisted that night.

Fig. 14. *Fort Laramie* by Alfred Jacob Miller. Wikimedia Commons.

Imagine Aaron's surprise when his younger brother, George, appeared at the fort the following spring. George, who had been suffering from malaria and severe malnourishment when Aaron abandoned the family the previous October, had also left the Martin Company, intending to return to the fort. Several days after Aaron enlisted, George sneaked away from his family undetected. But exhausted and in desperation, he instead stumbled, nearly dead, into the lodge of an Oglala family. George's father, who searched for the boy, found him there a few days later, still extremely sick but warm and fed. His father wanted to take him back to the company but soon recognized that George's only hope for survival rested in the hands of the Oglala woman who had been caring for him. George's father returned to the Martin Company without his son. This Indian family nursed George back to health over the winter. When spring came, he was well enough to make the trek to Fort Laramie, where he became a civilian cook for the army stationed there.

Fig. 15. *Fort Laramie Interior* by Alfred Jacob Miller. Wikimedia Commons.

Fort Laramie was one of a handful of forts constructed along the trails used by pioneers traveling west. These forts, built along both the overland trails and the waterways used by pioneers and merchants, played a vital role in supporting emigration and trade. They served as landmarks in an otherwise unbroken prairie. Travelers could resupply, make needed repairs to their wagons, and exchange their weary stock for fresh animals. The military presence at some forts was reassuring to pioneers, particularly during periods of conflict between emigrants and the Indigenous people whose existence was threatened by the intruders. Outlets directly associated with the forts were not the only source of supplies, however, as Indigenous, American, and European traders often set up their own shops near forts, hoping to attract some of the business. As with the Harrison brothers, the pioneers who crossed the Great Plains were influenced a great deal by the forts that served as trade emporiums along the major pioneer routes, including the Santa Fe Trail; the Oregon, Mormon, and California Trails; El Camino Real de los Tejas; and the Mississippi and Missouri Rivers.

The Santa Fe Trail

The Santa Fe Trail was an international commercial route that connected Franklin, Missouri, with the Spanish, and later Mexican, city of Santa Fe, a distance of almost 900 miles. The route was discovered by Spaniards in the late eighteenth century and popularized by William Becknell in the early 1820s after Mexico gained independence from Spain and welcomed trade with the United States. American merchants loaded wagons in Franklin with manufactured goods, such as cloth, silks, buttons, and knives. They traveled using one of two forks: the more popular Mountain Route, which followed the Arkansas River west before turning south along the eastern fringe of the Rocky Mountains, or the southern Cimarron Route, which was more direct but lacked water. At the end of their fifty-to-sixty-day journey, merchants sold both their wares and wagons, earning a huge profit in Santa Fe. They would then purchase inexpensive mules and travel back to Franklin loaded with silver coins and processed gold. Once in Missouri, they sold the mules for a large profit and purchased and outfitted a new caravan of wagons.

Commerce on the Santa Fe Trail was lucrative but hazardous. Comanche leaders demanded a payment to ensure safe travel across their traditional homelands. Still, travelers were a tempting target for Native raiders from many nations, especially as traffic along the trail increased, causing substantial harm to bison herds and other resources essential for the survival of Indigenous peoples. On the Cimarron Route, a lack of water threatened destruction; on the Mountain Route, the rocky terrain slowed

Fig. 16. Bent's Fort, view from above. Wikimedia Commons.

travel and battered merchants and their wares. Despite these risks, commerce on the Santa Fe Trail grew exponentially as increasing numbers of Americans and Mexicans realized the opportunity to amass wealth through international trade.

In 1833 Bent's Fort was constructed on the north bank of the Arkansas River along the Mountain Route of the Santa Fe Trail by a small group of trappers who were experienced in the western fur trade, Ceran St. Vrain and Charles and William Bent. They originally built the fort to facilitate the exchange of furs and hides between traders and the Kiowas, Southern Cheyennes, Comanches, Arapahos, and other Indian nations of the southern plains. As the only major permanent American outpost on the Santa Fe Trail, Bent's Fort also became an important refuge and emporium for commercial caravans.

Before the first adobe brick was in place, St. Vrain and his partners imagined an impressive and massive fortress, distinct from the small stockades that typically served as trading posts in the West. For travelers on the Santa Fe Trail, Bent's Fort was

Fig. 17. Ceran St. Vrain.
Courtesy History
Colorado, Denver, no.
89.451.3435.]

an impressive sight. Outer walls of solid adobe, 30 inches thick and 14 feet tall, enclosed a large courtyard. Dwelling rooms of similar construction fringed a large plaza. Round towers 18 feet tall on the northeast and southwest corners gave the fort an impregnable feel. Large, enclosed corrals to the south and east of the fort could secure hundreds of animals. And along the west wall, a second tier of rooms provided permanent quarters for the fort's owners and additional space for guests.

Visitors at Bent's Fort could stay in a comfortable room while the resident blacksmith or carpenter made repairs to their wagons. They could sip a glass of ice water on the veranda that surrounded the plaza or drink a harder beverage while enjoying a game of cards or billiards in the upstairs entertainment room. A tailor on the site might sell them a new buckskin shirt or

Fig. 18. Charles Bent (*left*) and William Bent. Portrait drawing of Charles Bent courtesy History Colorado, Denver, no. 89.451.3346. Photograph of William Bent courtesy History Colorado, Denver, no. 89.451.3349.

leggings. Other supplies stored in the fort's many warehouses were available for purchase. The iron-clad gate at the main entrance provided visitors with peace of mind. In 1833 Bent's Fort was an oasis of comfort, unmatched in size or commercial importance across the Great Plains. As the U.S. Army expanded its western presence, officials offered William Bent a sizable sum for the fort (perhaps as much as ten times the $4,000 paid for Fort Laramie). He refused the offer.

Bent's Fort was visited by many notable trappers and traders of the West. Kit Carson was a frequent guest and spent much of the summer at the fort. Jedediah Smith, Jim Beckwourth, and many others boarded there. In 1845 government explorer John C. Frémont and his party stopped at the fort on their way to California in a search for trails west. It was at Bent's Fort in 1846 that Susan Magoffin, en route to Santa Fe with her husband,

Samuel, suffered a miscarriage under the care of a physician. That same day a local Indian woman gave birth to a healthy baby at the fort, adding to her grief. Gen. Stephen Kearny used the fort as a staging area for the Army of the West in 1846 during the war with Mexico. And of course, the owners of the fort, the Bent brothers and Ceran St. Vrain, maintained a regular presence. Bent's Fort was truly a frontier outpost, bringing together a rich diversity of guests. European American traders, Native and Métis trappers and hunters, Mexican merchants, and French Canadian and British trappers all passed in and out of its gates.

The war with Mexico devastated trade along the Santa Fe Trail and dealt a serious financial blow to the owners of Bent's Fort. A cholera outbreak associated with the 1849 gold rush ravaged the Bents' Indigenous trade partners. Other Native nations, pinched by the ever-increasing emigrant traffic, disrupted trade. In the fall of 1849 the fort was emptied and evacuated, and William Bent burned and powdered the "castle of the plains" to the ground. Surprisingly, he built a new trading post nearby, much more modest in construction and scope. In 1853 he strengthened the post by constructing a stone perimeter. However, as trade continued to decline, he eventually leased Bent's New Fort to the U.S. Army, which added barracks and greater defenses and renamed it Fort Lyon. The flooding Arkansas River caused the army to abandon the fort permanently in 1867, having constructed a new Fort Lyon in a safer location.

Other forts along the Santa Fe Trail included Fort Larned (1859–78), Fort Zarah (1864–69), and Fort Mann (1847–48), all of which served a fundamentally different purpose than Bent's Old Fort did. They were built to house soldiers to protect the Santa Fe Trail and other American interests by intimidating and "chastising" the Native nations of the region. None could rival Bent's Old Fort for its construction or importance as an emporium during the richest years of Santa Fe Trail commerce.

The Oregon, California, and Mormon Trails

Unlike the commercial travel on the Santa Fe Trail, the primary use of the Oregon, California, and Mormon Trails was by emigrants looking to relocate to new homes in the West. Departing from Independence, Missouri, in April or May, the pioneers on the Oregon and California Trails hoped to reach their destinations in Oregon City, Sacramento, San Francisco, or Los Angeles by September or October. Travelers on the Mormon Trail, which followed nearly the same route as the Oregon and California Trails for much of the journey, typically left Council Bluffs, Iowa, in May and arrived in the Salt Lake Valley by late July (though the Martin Handcart Company did not leave Florence, Nebraska, until late August, which proved a deadly mistake). Travelers along these trails followed paths blazed by Indigenous peoples and "rediscovered" by fur trappers in the 1820s and 1830s. Although the pioneer trails had several jumping-off points, they converged at Fort Kearny and followed the same route along the Platte River across the western Great Plains. The trails diverged after reaching the Rocky Mountains in several "partings of the ways," based on the emigrants' final destinations.

Overland emigrant traffic commenced in 1841 and increased through the decades that followed, with Mormon pioneers joining the traffic in 1847 and miners bound for the goldfields of California in 1849. Estimates of the numbers of emigrants who traveled these overland trails before the completion of the transcontinental railroad in 1869 range from 350,000 to 500,000 souls. As they crossed the Great Plains, these courageous travelers found refuge in two major emporiums, Fort Kearny and Fort Laramie. A handful of other outposts dotted the trails at different times, and pioneers passed other major forts such as Fort Bridger and Fort Hall after entering the Rocky Mountains.

In 1848, as pioneer traffic on the Oregon and California Trails increased, Lt. Daniel P. Woodbury, under the direction of Stephen Kearny, established a military outpost named Fort Childs on the south bank of the Platte River in modern Nebraska. Located where the pioneer trails from Council Bluffs, Iowa; Independence and St. Joseph, Missouri; and other jumping-off points converged to form what was later called the Great Platte River Road, the military post was soon renamed Fort Kearny. The fort consisted of a handful of unfortified adobe and log warehouses, homes, and barracks that surrounded a four-acre parade ground. Soldiers planted cottonwood trees around the perimeter of the complex for shade. Woodbury and other commanders of the post were ordered to support emigration by selling supplies at cost, offering a place to rest, and providing mail service. A doctor was on site much of the time and could address the wide range of afflictions that pioneers suffered. Blacksmiths and carpenters were kept busy making repairs to wagons and other equipment.

In its first year, Fort Kearny became an important emporium on the emigrant trails. Pioneers heading west typically reached the fort in late May, about three weeks into their trek, a good time to rest, restock supplies, exchange their animals for fresh ones, and mail letters home. In 1849, the year of the California Gold Rush and Fort Kearny's first full year of operation, about four thousand wagons had stopped at the fort by June, when the spring traffic was winding down. The fort, still in its infancy, was not prepared for the onslaught of visitors that year. In fact, sometimes the soldiers stationed at the fort attempted to purchase supplies from travelers. "Both men and officers were ill off for some necessities, such as flour and sugar," the forty-niner William Kelly reported, "the privates being more particular in their inquiries after whiskey . . . but we had none to sell them even at [a] tempting price." Other travelers had more luck in purchasing necessities such as flour or whiskey while at the fort.

Within a few years, thousands of wagons stopped at the fort each day during the busy spring season. Over the next decades, soldiers stationed at the fort assumed a more active role in defending emigrants from attacks by Pawnee, Cheyenne, or Sioux warriors, as the Natives' lifestyle was threatened by the growing white presence on the plains. Supplies such as flour and pork were sometimes distributed from the fort to Native groups who were becoming more destitute as a result of white encroachment. At other times, Pawnee women visited the fort to try to sell dried bison meat to emigrants. A series of gold rushes to Colorado, Montana, and Nevada led to continued pioneer traffic through Fort Kearny. Freight traffic along the trail and through Fort Kearny fluctuated based on Native postures. Eventually, Fort Kearny became an important way station on the major stagecoach route across the plains. A Pony Express station was built at the fort.

With the construction of railroad lines crossing Nebraska, however, the usefulness of Fort Kearny as an emporium ended. In 1866, with many of its buildings in disrepair, Gen. William T. Sherman suggested that Fort Kearny be abandoned, though it took several years to act on his recommendation. The fort was formally closed in 1875.

FORT LARAMIE

One of the most important emporiums on the Oregon, California, and Mormon Trails was Fort Laramie. In the 1830s fur trapper William Sublette constructed Fort William, later known as Fort John on the Laramie and then simply Fort Laramie, near the confluence of the North Platte and Laramie Rivers. It was intended to serve as a fur-trading post to support trappers and hunters in the region. The site had long been known for its geographic and commercial importance, and earlier trading posts had been built in the same area, sometimes in competition with each other. In 1841 the original log fort was dismantled and replaced by an adobe structure. In the 1840s, when pioneers began to use the Great Platte River Road as part of the Oregon, California, and Mormon Trails, Fort Laramie became the principal trading depot in the central plains, rivaling Bent's Fort in popularity and economic significance. With the increasing emigration, the owners of the fort retooled it as an emporium, designed to resupply emigrant wagon trains, though it continued to facilitate trade in furs and bison hides as well.

Pioneers frequently spent a few days resting and regrouping at Fort Laramie, where they could mail letters home, purchase provisions, make needed wagon repairs, and exchange worn-out livestock for fresh animals. Mail sent from the fort reached the Missouri River in as little as twelve days. Some pioneers anticipated the opportunity to purchase supplies at the fort and traveled lightly during the first leg of the journey. Travelers who reached Fort Laramie knew that they had covered about a quarter of the trail to Oregon or California or half the trail to the Salt Lake Valley. They also knew that the most grueling stretch of the journey, through South Pass and across the Continental Divide, lay before them. Fort Laramie was a strategic site with plentiful pasturage where people and animals could rest before continuing across the high plains of Wyoming and through the Rocky Mountains.

In 1849 the U.S. government purchased Fort John on the Laramie for $4,000 from the American Fur Company and then shortened the name to Fort Laramie. The U.S. Army converted it into a military station, adding several buildings. By 1851 the fort compound included a stable large enough for eighty horses, officers' and soldiers' quarters, a sutler's store, saloon and pool hall, bakery, powder magazine, sawmill, blacksmith shop, workshops, and barracks for the quartermaster and his soldiers. The fort sat on a bluff overlooking the Laramie River. High adobe walls with square towers on the southwest and northeast corners added to its impressive appearance. With outer dimensions of 123 by 168 feet, the fort was divided in two by a partition, with storerooms, offices, and apartments around the perimeter of one side and a corral on the other. Along the west wall was a second tier of rooms. Two gates protected the fort's single entrance. It is little wonder that the Harrison boys in the Martin Handcart Company were impressed by what they saw when they rested at Fort Laramie in October 1856. The fort soon became the prairie home of both Aaron and George as they abandoned the starving pioneer company, with Aaron enlisting in the army and George serving as a civilian staff member for one of the fort's officers.

The fort continued to grow with the expanding pioneer traffic, resulting in tensions with Indians, who suffered severely as increasing numbers of emigrants brought diseases and devastated the wild animal herds they depended on for food. By 1867 the original fort was gone, replaced by the commanding officer's quarters. Additional barracks, a hospital, graveyard (next to the hospital), post office, laundries, and other buildings had been added to the complex. During the 1860s Fort Laramie assumed a greater role in the execution of the U.S. policy toward Natives. An important council was held at Fort Laramie in 1868, with U.S. officials and leaders of the various Sioux tribes agreeing to a peace treaty formally ending Red Cloud's war along the Bozeman Trail. The Treaty of Fort Laramie reserved the sacred Black Hills of South Dakota exclusively for the Sioux nation in perpetuity, an agreement that Americans violated less than a decade later.

In the 1870s changing conditions caused Fort Laramie to be retooled once again. The completion of the transcontinental railroad ended the pioneer era and the need for emporiums. In addition, as the U.S. government forced Indigenous groups onto reservations, conflicts between them and the American ranchers decreased. New threats like lawless cattle rustlers arose, creating a policing role for troops at the fort. And local settlers relied on the fort to obtain supplies from the East. But when railroad routes bypassed the fort to the south and north, its fate was sealed. In 1890 Fort Laramie closed, and its 35,000 acres of military reservation lands were opened to homesteading.

El Camino Real de los Tejas

El Camino Real de los Tejas, or the Royal Road of the Tejas, was one of the first European routes across the southern fringe of the Great Plains in central Texas. Tejas was the Spanish word for the Caddo Indians, a prominent nation in the region. The road linked Mexico City in the south with Natchitoches in modern Louisiana. This trade route, used by Indigenous peoples for centuries, became important in the late 1600s as Spain attempted to secure its northern territories. In later eras El Camino Real de los Tejas was used by Mexican, Texan, and American traders and pioneers, along with the Indians who blazed the trails.

Unsurprisingly, forts were established along the route, some of which were on the southern Great Plains. The most famous of these was the Alamo, built near the mission at San Antonio. In the 1820s, after Mexico gained its independence from Spain and allowed Anglo settlers to enter its territory, a stream of American pioneers followed El Camino Real de los Tejas into Texas, which was still part of Mexico. Forts that had once defended Spanish territory were now used to protect and resupply the welcomed American settlers.

After Texas's brief independence and annexation into the United States, Anglo settlement continued to advance west, with forts playing a central role in protecting travelers on an expanding network of pioneer routes. A southern emigrant trail, open year-round, linked eastern Texas with California through Santa Fe and across southern Arizona. Fort McKavett, Fort Concho, Fort Stockton, Fort Davis, Fort Quitman, and Fort Bliss defended emigrants and settlers in central Texas. Fort Griffin, Fort Richardson, Fort Sill (Oklahoma), and Fort Elliott defended pioneers entering northern Texas and Oklahoma. The Alamo and Fort McKavett serve as representative case studies of the roles of these forts in supporting travelers on El Camino Real de los Tejas and other pioneer routes across the Texas plains.

THE ALAMO

By the early 1700s Spain recognized the grave challenges it faced in preserving its holdings in Louisiana and eastern Texas and decided to build missions as way stations between Mexico City and the remote outposts to the north and east. Mission San Antonio de Valero, later called the Alamo, a fortified Spanish mission constructed near the headwaters of the San Antonio River, served as such a way station. Founded in 1718, the mission had grown in size and influence by the mid-1700s and was largely self-sufficient, with local Indian residents playing a substantial role in its success and defense against Apache and Comanche raiders.

The Alamo gained an increasingly fortresslike appearance and role with the addition of walls, a turret, and several cannons at strategic locations around the mission. While the mission was growing, a nearby community called San Antonio de Bexar, complete with its own fort, was also thriving, and travelers along El Camino Real de los Tejas could find respite here. Despite the investment in the mission's defenses, the Indigenous population at the Alamo declined in the late 1700s, and it was completely abandoned in 1793. But San Antonio maintained its importance as a way station for travelers in Spain's northern colonial realm.

A decade later, the Alamo, as it was then called, was reoccupied by military forces of Spain and then Mexico. The Alamo gained fame during Texas's war for independence from Mexico because of the battle fought there in 1836. Though its construction as a fort was somewhat haphazard, with its church never completed, and its role as a way station was overshadowed by the nearby settlement of San Antonio, the Alamo continues to be one of the most famous forts on El Camino Real de los Tejas.

FORT MCKAVETT

When gold was discovered in California, the California Trail across the central plains was only one of several routes that led to the goldfields. Some forty-niners chose to take a southern route across the plains of Texas to Santa Fe and on to California through southern Arizona. Increased emigrant travel through the region led government officials to decide to build a string of forts across the frontier of Texas to support and protect both emigrants and settlers from the Indigenous peoples, who contested the intrusions into their lands. Fort McKavett, built on the banks of the San Saba River in 1851, was one of several forts constructed along the Upper Road linking San Antonio in the east with Fort Bliss in western Texas.

Fort McKavett gradually gained a feeling of permanence on the frontier. Soldiers used quarried local stone to construct their own quarters and worked collaboratively to build the fort's headquarters and other common structures. Within five years the 2,000-acre complex included twenty-one stone buildings, among them several administrative buildings, soldier barracks, and a hospital. Supplies came to the fort from San Antonio at great expense because of the distance. Emigrants along the Upper Road could resupply there, though at high prices, as most of the freight shipped into the fort was intended for use by the troops stationed there.

Though the stone structures at Fort McKavett gave it the appearance of permanence, its usefulness proved to be short-lived. Many of the trail-weary emigrants bound for California saw the fertile Texas plains as a home more appealing than unknown landscapes far to the west. An increasing number of homesteaders settled in Texas and took up ranching or farming. Gradually, Americans pushed west as they sought more land and as Indian nations were decimated by disease, starvation, and military engagement. As settlers advanced westward, Fort McKavett became less important and closed in 1859.

Fort McKavett's closure proved temporary, however. During the Civil War, soldiers were pulled out of the frontier for combat in the eastern theater of the war. The Indian nations of western Texas took advantage of the absence of soldiers to resume raiding to perhaps reclaim their lands. When the Civil War ended, troops were again sent to Fort McKavett to protect a new wave of emigration and settlement. Under the command of Ranald Mackenzie, the ruins of the original fort were replaced by new stone structures. The African American Buffalo Soldiers under Mackenzie's command waged a relentless campaign against the Indian nations of the region. Fort McKavett became a vital supply depot, receiving freight from San Antonio and storing and shipping it to Fort Concho or other forts and outposts closer to the front lines of Indian combat.

Soldiers at Fort McKavett served in a variety of ways. For example, on May 16, 1870, two young brothers, Herman and Willie Lehman, were kidnapped by Apache raiders near the fort. Buffalo Soldier Emanuel Stance was sent with a patrol four days later to attempt to rescue the boys. Stance and his men found the guilty raiding party about 14 miles north of Fort McKavett. The soldiers charged the Apaches, firing their repeating rifles into the raiders' encampment. While the Apaches fought back, Willie Lehman escaped. Stance's party launched other attacks that were successful in retaking captured horses, but they were unable to rescue Herman Lehman, who lived for several years with the Apaches and Comanches before gaining his freedom. Emanuel Stance was awarded the Medal of Honor for his gallantry, the first African American to receive this honor for action taken during the Indian Wars.

Fort McKavett was abandoned a second time in 1883. Soon families and businesses moved into the empty structures. Within a few years, a small but thriving community had developed. Interestingly, this town served one of the same purposes as the original fort—supplying the neighboring farmers and ranchers with needed goods.

The Mississippi and Missouri Rivers

Much of the travel into the Old Northwest and the West occurred by river rather than road. Trade goods and supplies could be shipped more cheaply and easily by boat than by wagon. The Mississippi and Missouri Rivers served as arteries of trade and travel onto and across the Great Plains. And just as forts served as emporiums on land routes, they also facilitated travel and trade at key locations on the river systems. Like Bent's Old Fort on the Santa Fe Trail and Fort Laramie on the Oregon Trail, Fort Benton, Fort Snelling, and others were originally built to facilitate trade with Indians and defend U.S. interests on the frontier. But with the increasing Anglo presence in the Old Northwest and on the northern plains of Montana and Alberta, some of these forts served additional purposes as supply emporiums for emigrants and settlers and as military staging areas. Forts were sited at strategic locations, often at the confluence of major rivers or the most remote point where river navigation was possible. Fort Armstrong, Fort Crawford, Fort Snelling, and other military forts were constructed along the Mississippi River in the 1810s, complementing the string of privately operated fur-trading posts that came to dot the eastern edge of the Great Plains. Fort Union and Fort Benton were fur-trading outposts built on the Missouri River that were later used by the military to support emigration and settlement. Fort Snelling and Fort Benton are representative examples of river emporiums.

FORT SNELLING

For generations, Natives had inhabited a village on the high bluff overlooking a place that the Dakotas called Bdóte, the confluence of the Minnesota and Mississippi Rivers. When American explorer Zebulon Pike viewed the site, he immediately recognized its strategic importance and began talks with the Dakotas to use the land for a military post. The Dakota negotiators saw the benefits of having a post to facilitate trade within their territory. Soon a treaty was concluded, though its legitimacy was later questioned by Dakota signatories. Even Pike was not satisfied with the meager payment the United States made for the use of the land. Still, in 1819 the U.S. Army began constructing a cantonment, called New Hope, on the flats near the confluence of the rivers. Within a year, after a terrible winter where many soldiers perished from scurvy and other ailments, the army post was relocated to the bluff overlooking the rivers and renamed Fort St. Anthony, after the nearby St. Anthony Falls on the Mississippi River. Construction continued for several years. In 1825 the fort was renamed Fort Snelling in honor of its second commander and primary architect.

Over the next decades, the original wooden buildings of the fort were replaced by limestone structures using materials quarried from the riverbanks. The fort was enclosed by a 9-foot-tall stone wall forming a diamond shape. Two block-houses overlooked the rivers, and a round watchtower rose above the point of the confluence. A lookout tower on the opposite end of the fort gave sentinels a view of the open prairie to the west. A boat landing was constructed directly below the bluff, and eventually a stairway and a less direct wagon road meandered from the river up to the fort. Within the walls of the fort were army barracks, mess rooms, kitchens, and quar-ters for the officers, laundresses, paymaster, and others. There were also rooms for storage, a post school, and a hospital. A guardhouse protected both sides of the gated entrance, and a large parade area occupied the middle of the fort. Outside the fort's walls to the west were the buildings of an Indian agency, a blacksmith shop that catered to the needs of Natives, and the home of the post's sutler. Near the fort, the village of Mendota sprang to life, a collection of trading houses built by Anglos and Indigenous people to attract the business of those who visited the fort. At its center was a trading post operated by the American Fur Company. The surrounding area soon had a sawmill, gristmill, Catholic chapel, and cemetery.

During the early years of Fort Snelling's existence, goods were delivered to the fort from St. Louis by flatboats and keelboats. Even after the development of steamboats, flatboats that could navigate shallow water were still often used, as the river depth fluctuated based on the annual precipitation. Supplies could not be delivered by flatboat or steamboat during the winter months when the rivers were covered with ice. The sutler at Fort Snel-ling offered goods at prices fixed by policy to prevent him from taking advantage of his monopoly. Accounts kept by Franklin Steele, the sutler from 1838 to 1858, show that his store offered a wide variety of products. Soldiers might purchase fresh cur-rants or raisins, shoes, soap, apples, butter, cider, indigo, paper, cheese, suspenders, needles, sugar, tin cups, cloves, pepper, scrub brushes, brooms, candy, and even fishing tackle. In the case of alcohol, the fort served the purpose of blocking rather than facilitating trade. In 1832 a policy was enforced prohibiting the sale of alcohol to Indians. Thereafter ships passing the fort were searched, and alcohol, if found, was seized and destroyed or stored at the fort.

Fort Snelling represented U.S. governmental authority near the remote but strategic Mississippi headwaters region. At various times the fort lay within the territorial boundaries of Upper Louisiana, Michigan, Wisconsin, Iowa, and Minnesota. In the 1840s, as railroads linked eastern cities with the Mississippi River and steamboats provided access to the Old Northwest, Fort Snelling became a popular tourist attraction, drawing visitors who traveled by steamboat from St. Louis or Galena. These visitors to Minnesota's frontier primarily wanted to see the St. Anthony Falls on the Mississippi River and the nearby Minnehaha Falls, but they were also impressed by Fort Snelling's location and impregnable appearance on the bluff overlooking the rivers. Visitors' reports inspired emigration to Minnesota.

Fort Snelling served a much more important purpose than simply being a tourist attraction. Originally constructed to strengthen the U.S. claim and presence in the Old Northwest, the fort became the hub from which the Anglo settlement of Minnesota and the Old Northwest radiated. In 1821 the first settlers arrived and built homes near the fort. Soldiers from Fort Snelling promoted settlement in the region by employing and actively trading with local civilians. The physician at the fort served settlers in the area. Discharged soldiers from Fort Snelling often joined the ranks of the settlers, taking up farming near the fort.

In the 1840s publishers began to release emigrant guides to Minnesota. In one, *Rural Sketches of Minnesota, the El Dorado of the Northwest*, Henry W. Hamilton praised what he saw during a visit: "Yes, I am in Minnesota. It seems like a dream, almost: and yet I am in the very midst of a world of deeply interesting realities.... Bright skies are above me; glorious scenery is around me; 'the Father of Waters,' mighty and majestic as when Time was young, is roaring and sweeping on below me; the images of a beautiful land, a new El Dorado, are seen on every side; the impulses of a young empire, mighty while young, and ambitious ... are thrilling every heart and quickening every pulse." Hamilton praised the pure air and water, the broad rolling prairies, the flourishing villages, and the prosperous businesses. He argued that "no where are farmers making money faster and easier than in Minnesota." Fort Snelling played a prominent role in Hamilton's visit and in the lives of the emigrants who answered his call to come to the El Dorado of the Northwest.

Although there were no mass migrations to Minnesota, the consistent and gradual emigration to the region drastically changed the landscape over time. Emigrants were supplied with goods shipped by steamboat up the Mississippi River from St. Louis and unloaded at Fort Snelling for distribution. In its early years, the fort was used as a distribution center for gifts and provisions to the Indigenous peoples, whose resources were destroyed by increasing American settlement. Later, the fort served as an emporium of supplies used by emigrants embarking from Fort Snelling or settlers of the region. Eventually, goods were warehoused and distributed by private interests established in two nearby communities, St. Paul and Minneapolis. By 1849, with increasing Anglo settlement in the region, Fort Snelling was no longer on the frontier. The territorial capital was relocated from Fort Snelling to nearby St. Paul, and the military capital was moved up the Mississippi River to Fort Gains, on the new frontier. Nine years later, in 1858, troops were removed from Fort Snelling, and it was closed. The fort was later reopened and used for a variety of purposes over the next century. But during the nearly forty years of its original existence, from 1819 to 1858, Fort Snelling served as an important trade emporium, facilitating the settlement of Minnesota and the Old Northwest.

FORT BENTON

Fort Benton served a similar role as Fort Snelling, but on the opposite edge of the Great Plains, in western Montana. Using building materials from nearby Fort Lewis, which was being dismantled, private investors began construction on Fort Benton in 1846. The fort was completed the following year. The trading post was on the north side of the Missouri River, according to the wishes of the Blackfeet Indians, the post's primary trade partners. Fort Benton was located at the farthest navigable point of the Missouri River. At almost 3,500 miles from the Gulf of Mexico, the fort has been called the "world's innermost port." In the early years of its existence, supplies were delivered to Fort Benton in barges, sometimes powered by wind but more often poled or drawn by rivermen using ropes. Within a decade of its construction, however, lighter-weight "mountain" steamboats were designed with a lower draft that enabled them to travel in shallow water. After 1860 goods could be shipped to Fort Benton relatively inexpensively, and from there they were distributed throughout the region.

One of the owners of Fort Benton visited Fort John (Laramie) in 1850 and was impressed by its adobe construction. He decided to give Fort Benton a similar makeover, renovating it over the next decade by removing its wooden structures and rebuilding using adobe. The renovation was completed in 1860, the same year in which the first mountain steamboats visited the fort. Unfortunately, the *Chippewa*, one of the first steamboats on the Upper Missouri River, caught fire and exploded on its way to Fort Benton, sending a shower of trade goods onto Anglo travelers and Crow and Sioux observers of the accident.

In 1862 word of recent mineral discoveries in Montana triggered a gold rush to the region. Fort Benton became a growing community that served as an emporium for trade goods available to emigrants passing through the region as well as to the settlers who called the area home. Miners brought healthy appetites, and as bison herds diminished, cattle herds grazed in their place. Ranching became a thriving economic activity in the region surrounding Fort Benton, creating an increasing demand for the manufactured goods brought by steamboat. One of the trade goods in highest demand was whiskey, some of which was delivered on the Whoop-Up Trail across the Canadian border into Alberta to Fort Hamilton, also known as Fort Whoop-Up. This illegal trade in whiskey flourished until the arrival of North-West Mounted Police in 1873. The decline of the illicit whiskey trade had little impact on the importance of Fort Benton as an emporium, however.

Between 1860 and 1890 about 160,000 tons of supplies and over forty thousand passengers were delivered by steamboat to Fort Benton, from where they went by overland freight to the fledgling communities and mining camps of northern Montana and southern Alberta. Fort Benton also served as a warehouse for bison hides, furs, gold, and other raw materials that were brought in by local Blackfeet trappers and hunters, ranchers, farmers, and miners. During those same decades, about 35,000 tons of goods, including 750,000 bison robes, 120 tons of gold, horses, cattle, and millions of pounds of wool, were shipped out of Fort Benton by the same steamboats that delivered manufactured goods there. Today Fort Benton is considered the first permanent American settlement in the state of Montana, though its population has increased little since its founding and early growth.

Forts like those described in this chapter served an important role as emporiums on the emigration and trade routes that transformed the Great Plains from Indian lands to frontier to Anglo settlements. Though each fort was unique in its construction and particular influence, collectively they contributed to breaking down Native self-sufficiency while promoting American economic and transportation interests. Each fort stored supplies that helped pioneers survive their treks and improved the lives of those who settled within trading distance of their walls. Further, they contributed to the lore of the northern, southern, western, and eastern Great Plains.

CHAPTER FOUR

Military Outposts

In April 1870 Fort Concho, a new military outpost in central Texas, was the site of the funeral and burial of Lucy Getchell Merriam. Four years earlier Lucy had married Henry C. Merriam, veteran of the Civil War and soon to be commander of Fort Bayard in New Mexico Territory. Lucy accompanied her husband on his adventure into the West, giving birth to a daughter, Mamie, who spent her first years moving with her parents from fort to fort. On the evening of April 24, while the family was traveling from Fort Bliss to Fort McKavett in Texas, tragedy struck. Henry Merriam's command had established a camp near the confluence of the North and Middle Concho Rivers. Henry reviewed the troops in the evening and returned to his tent, finding all well. He recounted in his report of the tragedy, "I had been out, and returned about eight, finding my darlings in bed, Mamie asleep. Mrs. M. said Mamie had said her little prayer followed by her usual 'goodnight mama, goodnight papa,' and then added 'Mama, I want to go find papa,' and dropped off to sleep."

Henry lay down beside his wife, but before he could fall asleep, he heard the sound of an approaching storm. He dressed, checked to make certain his tent was secure, and waited for the storm to hit. When the tempest arrived, it brought a combination of rain and hail, with hailstones the size of eggs. The downpour woke Lucy, and she lifted the startled Mamie into her arms. Eventually, Henry peeked out and saw that a nearby creek had risen to the edge of their tent and was continuing to swell. He called for his escort, who, with the swift-flowing water rapidly rising, assisted Lucy and little Mamie into a carriage. Together with Henry on foot, they hurried toward higher ground. As they were about to reach safety, the rushing water swept Henry off his feet. Soldiers who were also fleeing the rising water arrived with their horses to aid him. But the carriage proved to be immovable. As Henry reached to help his wife and young daughter get out, the force of the raging flood pulled him downstream. He struggled against the current and debris and eventually reached the shore, where, to his horror, he was informed that the carriage had rolled over and tumbled out of sight. Soldiers at the scene said they had heard Lucy calmly say her final words: "My darling husband, goodbye." As the deluge continued, there was nothing he could do that night.

The next morning at about nine he found the bodies of several soldiers and his wife, who had perished in the flood. He recalled, "I took from the water with my own hands, my darling wife's body! Cold—Cold and dead!" He described the expression of terror frozen on her face, which miraculously "changed to one of sweet, smiling slumber" as he tenderly prepared her for burial. After a futile search for his little Mamie, he turned his back on the site of the tragedy, expecting never to see her again. But two days later Mamie's lifeless body was discovered 4 miles below camp, and she was buried with her mother at Fort Concho. "Thus they are both gone," Henry lamented. "The gentle vine and tenderest bud which clung so sweetly about my life, softening every care, and sweetening every pleasure, ruthlessly torn away without a moment's notice."

Fig. 19. Henry C. Merriam. Courtesy Library of Congress.

Fort Concho, near the site of the tragedy, was one of scores of forts that dotted the Great Plains, serving as military outposts from the seventeenth through the twenty-first centuries. Wherever they were constructed, forts played a central role in the lives of soldiers and officers and their families, emigrants and settlers, Indians and miners, railroad workers and stagecoach drivers, preachers and ranchers. Forts contained homes, stores, stables, schools, churches, blacksmith shops, corrals, and funeral parlors. For thousands who died in combat, epidemics, or accidents, such as befell Lucy and Mamie Merriam, forts served as a final resting place. Ultimately, military outposts were constructed to meet national objectives. The purposes of such posts, sponsored, staffed, and administered by national governments, changed over time.

During the first three hundred years of European interest in the Great Plains, military outposts sent a message to rival nations and resident Indians about imperial claims to the land and provided an indication of their intent to remain (see the introduction). A handful of Spanish presidios, such as Presidio San Saba in Texas, and French forts, such as Fort de Cavagnial in modern-day Kansas, served these purposes. After the United States gained its independence, military outposts on the frontier of the Great Plains protected emigrants, commercial interests, transportation and communication lines, and settlers. Later, forts constructed by the U.S. government served as recruiting and training centers for Union and Confederate armies. Forts were used as quarters and defensive strongholds during the Indian Wars of the postbellum nineteenth century. In the twentieth century, both during and after the world wars, forts continued to serve as locations where troops could be housed and trained and military equipment could be built or stored. In this chapter, we consider each of these eras of U.S. military outpost construction.

Protecting Emigrants

In the mid-nineteenth century, as American settlers began to pour into the West, the U.S. government perceived the necessity of patrolling pioneer trails and invested in the construction of outposts or purchased existing forts at strategic locations along each trail. Secretary of War John Calhoun, an ardent supporter of national expansion, conceived of an ambitious plan to connect the fortifications on the Great Lakes with new ones on the Upper Missouri. He authorized the Yellowstone Expedition to ascend the Missouri and construct a fort near the confluence of the Yellowstone and Missouri Rivers to protect the American fur trade in 1819. Unfortunately, transportation difficulties with the steamboats, unforeseeable delays, enormous costs, and opposition from Congress combined to detain the expedition on the west bank of the Missouri, a short distance above the present-day city of Omaha, Nebraska. The expedition members abandoned their plans to proceed upstream and instead erected Cantonment Missouri, soon relocated 2 miles south to the top of a bluff overlooking the river and renamed Fort Atkinson. Fort Atkinson functioned as the most important western military post on the Middle Missouri for almost a decade, until the construction of Fort Leavenworth in Kansas in 1827.

From the 1820s through the 1860s the number of military outposts on the Great Plains multiplied as increasing numbers of pioneers and miners headed west. For example, Fort Leavenworth was constructed in 1827 to defend the eastern portion of the Santa Fe Trail from its origin in Franklin, Missouri; Fort Marcy was built in 1846 to protect its western segment and terminus in Santa Fe; and Fort Atkinson was established to safeguard travelers along western trails. In the case of Fort Atkinson, there were no trees for many miles, so the fort was limited to sod structures, which quickly fell into disrepair and were abandoned within three years. In 1854 the outpost was reestablished, though without any buildings. The soldiers briefly stationed there protected a makeshift mail station and travelers through the summer, but they abandoned the outpost that October. The need to defend emigrants and merchants passing through central Kansas did not diminish, however, and from 1859 to 1878 soldiers in Fort Larned protected those on the Santa Fe Trail. A few years later, Fort Dodge added to the military presence on the Santa Fe Trail in Kansas, and Fort Lyon safeguarded travelers in eastern Colorado.

Similarly, forts were constructed to protect emigrants on the Oregon, California, and Mormon Trails. Unlike Fort Atkinson, Fort Kearny in modern-day Nebraska had a more permanent presence. Founded in 1848 in response to the growing traffic along the Platt River, Fort Kearny served as a source of provisions and protection for travelers. During the gold rush, its mission was magnified, with throngs of forty-niners resupplying there. One forty-niner, Edward Jackson, a prospective miner from Massachusetts on his way to the California goldfields, was not impressed by Fort Kearny when he first saw it on June 8, 1849. He disparaged it in his journal: "Fort Kearney is situated on the Platte [River]. It does not appear at all like a fort but is merely a few mud houses." Indeed, although called a fort, it lacked a stockade or any fortifications. In fact, only during the gravest of the Indian Wars in the mid-1860s were defensive earthworks constructed. Despite Jackson's disappointment, his party tarried at the fort for half a day while they repaired their wagons.

As traffic along the trail increased, so did the number of structures at Fort Kearny. Sod and adobe buildings were replaced by wooden frame structures. In 1860 the fort had a Pony Express station. Later, a telegraph station was included among the thirty buildings of its expanding grounds. With the completion of the transcontinental railroad and the passing of the pioneer era, the military abandoned the fort, and neighbors disassembled and repurposed the building materials elsewhere.

Originally constructed by mountain man Robert Campbell in the mid-1830s, Fort Laramie in present-day eastern Wyoming represented the principal military outpost on the Oregon, California, and Mormon Trails. The U.S. Army purchased the fort in 1849 to protect emigrants along the overland trails. Unlike Fort Kearny, Fort Laramie had heavy fortifications, with a growing number of buildings surrounding the adobe and timber stockade. Jackson reached Fort Laramie on June 25 and recorded a brief description: "The fort formed a hollow square of 100 feet. The walls about 20 [feet] high. It may perhaps form a good fortification to keep the Indians in order but it is an ill looking place." It may not have looked like much in 1849, but an 1867 sketch shows that many structures had sprung up in and around the fort to improve the comfort of those stationed there. A footbridge gave soldiers and travelers access to the structures on both sides of the river. Indian lodges often encircled the fort.

Fort Laramie rarely assumed a combative stance but more generally served to house soldiers and supply settlers. By 1890, when the fort was abandoned and the materials were sold to local settlers, more than fifty buildings dotted the site. For many years Fort Laramie served as the only permanent military outpost between Fort Kearny and Fort Bridger in present-day southwestern Wyoming, an 800-mile stretch of the most heavily traveled pioneer trails.

Forts that had originally been constructed to defend emigrants were instrumental in the development of transportation and communication innovations that later linked East and West. The Butterfield Overland Mail Company, operating from

1857 to 1861, blazed a route across the southern plains, using military outposts such as Fort Belknap in Texas as stations and for protection. Stagecoaches and freight wagons stopped at plains forts, aiding their delivery of mail, passengers, and goods between St. Louis and San Francisco. Financial problems, cutthroat competition, and the outbreak of the Civil War stopped some of these ventures. In 1860, with the founding of the Pony Express mail delivery, forts such as Fort Kearny and Fort Laramie became important way stations, along with the many other small structures that served solely as Pony Express stations. In less than two years, however, the Pony Express became obsolete with the completion of the transcontinental telegraph, which followed roughly the same route and formed a communications link between the Atlantic and the Pacific Coasts. Fort Kearny and Fort Laramie both housed telegraph stations along the route. Just as the military outposts of the Great Plains had protected emigrants and miners, they also defended the transportation and communication networks that crossed the plains.

Military Outposts and the Civil War

The Great Plains stretch across three territories or states that were claimed by the Confederacy during the Civil War: Texas, Indian Territory (Oklahoma), and the eastern edge of New Mexico Territory. Federal military outposts in these regions generally fell temporarily into Confederate hands. Forts across the plains in both the North and South were used for recruiting and training. Military outposts in the central and northern Great Plains saw minimal combat during the Civil War but were important recruiting and training centers. At Fort Leavenworth, recruits from Kansas were inducted and trained. Fort Kearny and Fort Randall in modern-day South Dakota were left virtually unoccupied and saw little action as U.S. troops were relocated to the eastern theater of war.

Several forts in the south and west, however, did see action. Fort Davis in western Texas was constructed in 1854 and named for then secretary of war Jefferson Davis. Before the Civil War, the soldiers stationed at Fort Davis defended settlers from the powerful Comanche, Kiowa, and Apache Nations. Federal troops evacuated Fort Davis when Texas seceded from the Union in 1861. It was soon occupied by Confederate troops, who resumed the work of their northern predecessors, pursuing Indians. In the summer of 1862 Union forces chased the Confederate soldiers out of the fort and briefly took possession. Finding little use in deploying manpower to hold this frontier fort, the Union soon abandoned the post, and it remained unoccupied until the end of the Civil War.

Perhaps the most important attempt by Confederate forces to seize a federally controlled plains fort occurred at Fort Union along the Santa Fe Trail in eastern New Mexico. Built by Lt. Col. Edwin V. Sumner in 1851 at the junction of the Mountain and Cimarron branches of the Santa Fe Trail, Fort Union represented a traditional fort designed to protect mail, commerce, and travelers. When news of an impending invasion of New Mexico Territory by Texan Confederates surfaced in 1861, soldiers worked day and night to erect a new Fort Union east of the original fort. Constructed in the Mora valley, it was designed to withstand a siege and defend the water supply at Wolf Creek. This massive bastioned defensive earthwork contained parapets in the shape of an eight-pointed star. Each parapet offered a platform for artillery, and each star contained barracks, a storehouse, and officers' quarters.

The Texan army led by Big. Gen. Henry H. Sibley marched north up the Rio Grande valley and captured Albuquerque and the territorial capital of Santa Fe. Fort Union remained the only federal stronghold standing in the Confederacy's way of capturing the Colorado goldfields and Denver. Colorado volunteers and Union troops joined together and traveled south to meet the advancing army at Glorieta Pass between Santa Fe and Pecos. During the three-day battle on March 26–28, 1862, Union soldiers under Col. John P. Slough and the First Colorado Volunteers under Bvt. Maj. John M. Chivington successfully repelled and defeated the Confederates' advance, burned their supply wagons, and forced Sibley and his troops to retreat home to Texas. This Union victory stopped the advance and ended the Confederate threat to the region. Some historians consider this battle a lesser but still important western equivalent to Gen. George Meade's Army of the Potomac stopping the advance of Confederate general Robert E. Lee's Army of Northern Virginia in July 1863 at Gettysburg, Pennsylvania.

The second Fort Union is the sole surviving earthen star fort erected west of the Mississippi and is the most intact Civil War–era bastioned, earthen fort anywhere in the United States. After the Battle of Glorieta, the U.S. Army built a third Fort Union of territorial-style adobe brick laid on stone foundations. Constructed near the western border of the southwestern plains, and remaining in operation until 1891, this third Fort Union was the largest nineteenth-century military fort in the region. In 1954 the site became the Fort Union National Monument.

Meanwhile, southern sympathizers built a second Fort Davis in Indian Territory (future Oklahoma) to block a Union invasion and try to maintain the precarious loyalty of Natives to the Confederate cause. Also named for Jefferson Davis, president of the Confederate States of America at the time of its construction in 1861, this Fort Davis served as a Confederate headquarters in Indian Territory. Following the Union victory at Pea Ridge, Arkansas, in the spring of 1862, the Confederate army abandoned the fort, which had no stockade and consisted of only a handful of buildings. Union troops, including the

Third Indian Home Guard, briefly occupied the fort before burning it to ashes in December 1862.

Confederate Native troops, in the meantime, had relocated into the Choctaw Nation and erected Fort McCulloch in present-day Oklahoma. The fort remained in Confederate hands until the end of the war. For a brief period, Cherokee Confederate general Stand Watie used Fort McCulloch as his headquarters for the Regiment of Cherokee Mounted Rifles or Cherokee Braves, a military unit consisting of mixed-race Cherokees, Muskogee (Creek), and Seminoles, many of whom operated plantations, owned enslaved individuals, and supported and fought for the Confederacy. Lee's surrender to Grant at Appomattox Court House on April 9 officially ended the Civil War. Watie holds the distinction of being the last Confederate general in the field to surrender, which he did several months later, on June 23, 1865.

The Indian Wars

ON THE SOUTHERN PLAINS

Five years after Lucy and Mamie Merriam perished in the flash flood near Fort Concho, widower Henry Merriam, now commanding Fort Brown on the plains of southern Texas, was invited to a social call across the Mexican border in Matamoros. There he was introduced to twenty-five-year-old Catherine Una Macpherson MacNeil, a young woman who, according to one biographer, may have reminded him of his beloved Lucy. The following year Fort Brown was the site of their wedding. Merriam's bride explained, "There were many reasons for making a wedding easier on the American side [of the border]. Colonel Merriam had many friends in the regiment, to which he belonged for some time; they quite insisted we should be married at the Fort as it was really the best and pleasantest way, so we were married there by the army chaplain, many friends from Matamoros, as well as Brownsville being present." The military outposts of the Great Plains served many purposes, including as the wedding chapel for the couple.

The primary purpose of the military outposts in the post-bellum nineteenth century, however, was to defend American interests against Indian nations that opposed encroachment onto their lands. On the southern plains, the powerful nations of the Kiowas and Comanches proved formidable barriers to American expansion. During Henry Merriam's first expedition into the West in 1867, troops he led were met by a large group of Kiowa warriors. He later described the encounter during which he believed he had engaged Satanta, a Kiowa war chief: "These Indians were all armed with breech loading carbines, revolvers, and bows all of which they used according to circumstances during the skirmish. Their chief was mounted on a pony peculiarly spotted, and which was recognized by wagonmaster Thomas of my train as a favorite pony of Satanta, Chief of the Kiowas." He continued, "The manner in which they covered their retreat would have done credit to disciplined troops, while their skill in the management of their horses, entirely without the use of their arms, was wonderful."

By the time Merriam headed west in 1867, conflict between Comanches, Kiowas, and Apaches and Anglo and Mexican settlers had been going on for decades and increased as growing numbers of settlers encroached on Indian lands during the years following Texas's independence. Later, after the U.S. annexation of Texas in 1846, a system of forts was constructed there to protect settlers and defend transportation routes across the southern plains. Between 1846 and 1860 scores of forts, including Fort Belknap, Fort Clark, Fort Davis, Fort Lancaster, Fort McKavett, Fort Ringgold, and Fort Brown, the site of Merriam's wedding, were constructed.

Military outposts on the southern plains near the Mexican border served yet another purpose: to protect American interests against cattle rustlers and Mexican revolutionaries who frequently raided north of the border. Forts were often locations where several diverse cultures came together in clashes or in cooperation. The success of African American troops during the Civil War led Congress to create all-Black regiments, including the Ninth Cavalry Regiment, which occupied Texas forts and engaged in the Indian Wars of western Texas through the 1860s–70s and the conflicts with the Crow Nation in the 1880s. African American troops who battled the Indian nations of the plains were called Buffalo Soldiers because their hair reminded Indians of the hair on a buffalo's head. White officers who superintended African American regiments sometimes discriminated against them, though their grit in combat was never questioned. Moreover, forts attracted some Natives who saw the benefits of peaceful interaction with soldiers, settlers, and emigrants. Further, forts attracted Mexican traders and raiders, who added to the diversity of both friends and enemies.

ON THE CENTRAL AND NORTHERN PLAINS

In 1851 Fort Laramie, in present-day Wyoming, served as the location for a great peace conference. Representatives from the Arapaho, Arikara, Assiniboine, Cheyenne, Crow, Hidatsa, Mandan, and Sioux Nations met with treaty commissioners from the United States to end what had been years of escalating misunderstandings. The resulting treaty secured peace among the tribes and between American settlers and soldiers and Indian nations. It guaranteed the United States the right to build roads across and forts on Indian lands in return for annual payments. It defined the boundaries between tribes and included a pledge to end raiding and other depredations. For a time, conflicts decreased. As increasing numbers of settlers and miners encroached on Indian lands in violation of the treaty, however, fighting resumed and intensified in the 1860s. While the Civil War raged in the East, volunteers who lacked the training and discipline of professional soldiers manned the forts of the West, with catastrophic effects for the Natives. Often locally raised, filled with animosity toward Indians, and itching for the glory generally reserved for heroes of Civil War battlefields, many of these territorial militias were eager to fight and kill Indians at the slightest provocation or even without cause.

Colorado volunteers stationed at Fort Lyon under the command of John Chivington contributed to the escalating violence. In 1864 peaceful Cheyenne and Arapaho families had relocated near Fort Lyon in accordance with an agreement reached earlier that year. Meanwhile, a more militant band of the Cheyennes, known as Dog Soldiers, continued to harass American emigrants and take women and children captive. On November 29 a group of 675 volunteers under Chivington's command attacked the peaceful Cheyenne and Arapaho village at Big Sandy Creek, brutally killing as many as 160 people, about two-thirds of whom were women, children, and elderly men. This event became known as the Sand Creek Massacre. In response, most Cheyenne survivors united with Lakota Sioux and Arapaho warriors in a renewed fight against the American presence on the Great Plains.

Indigenous Americans rarely launched full-scale attacks against U.S. military outposts, whether staffed by trained soldiers or volunteers. A harsh winter, poor hunting conditions, and supply chain disruption of promised annuity provisions during the Civil War, however, led to starvation, hardship, and tension in North Dakota. In August 1862 Dakota Santee Sioux warriors led by Chief Little Crow attacked Fort Abercrombie and the Lower Sioux Agency on the eastern border of present-day North Dakota. Citizen soldiers, a regiment of African Americans, and nearby settlers who had fled to the fort for protection repulsed the Santees' initial attack, which was intended to drive settlers out of the Minnesota River valley. For six weeks Fort Abercrombie lay under siege, with warriors mounting full-scale assaults from time to time. Dakota warriors attacked and killed 358 settlers, seventy-seven soldiers, and twenty-nine members of the volunteer militia. The number of Dakota casualties remains unknown. Col. Henry Hastings Sibley finally defeated Little Crow at the Battle of Wood Lake on September 23. After the battle, hundreds of Dakotas surrendered. A military commission sentenced 303 Dakotas to death. President Abraham Lincoln commuted the sentences of all but 38 of those men, who were hanged in Mankato, Minnesota, on December 26, 1862, in the largest one-day mass execution in American history.

Forts were central to U.S. objectives during the escalating war being waged between the Lakota Sioux, Cheyennes, and Arapahos and the United States. After the discovery of gold in Montana in the early 1860s, John M. Bozeman and other miners blazed a route connecting the mining camps from Colorado's Front Range to those in Montana. The Bozeman Trail diverged from the Oregon Trail about 50 miles west of Fort Laramie and headed northwest, skirting the eastern edge of the Rocky Mountains.

The 1851 Treaty of Fort Laramie had a provision that enabled the military to construct military posts along emigrant trails in exchange for a $50,000 annuity to be paid annually for fifty years. The Senate reduced the treaty's duration to fifteen years. In 1866 diplomats met with Red Cloud to extend the treaty and receive permission to construct forts along the new miners' route to Montana. Initially, Red Cloud had considered agreeing to the terms. But when the construction crews arrived to build the forts with or without Lakota permission, Red Cloud changed his mind and refused to sign the 1866 treaty.

Red Cloud warned the military that the Lakota Nation did not approve of emigrants trespassing through their hunting grounds between the Yellowstone and Platte Rivers and that they intended to defend their homeland against any forts built on Lakota land. Despite the warnings, nearly thirty-five hundred emigrants traveled the trail between 1863 and 1868. Close to one hundred of them never reached their destination, killed by Lakotas defending their homeland and sovereignty. The army forged ahead with its fort construction plans, erecting Fort Reno and Fort Phil Kearny in present-day Wyoming and Fort C. F. Smith in southern Montana to defend miners and suppliers traveling the Bozeman Trail.

In July 1866 mountaineer Jim Bridger guided Col. Henry B. Carrington from Fort Laramie to Piney Creek to construct Fort Phil Kearny. Carrington had insufficient time to train his troops, limited supplies, and outdated muzzleloaders with little ammunition to spare. Hence, he proceeded cautiously. Troops under his command met mounting opposition to the construction of the forts. Red Cloud and Crazy Horse led other Lakotas, Northern Cheyennes, and Northern Arapahos in harassing the trains hauling lumber to the fort throughout the fall and winter.

On December 21, 1866, Crazy Horse led Lakota warriors in an attack on the fort's wood train. Capt. William J. Fetterman had chafed under Carrington's leadership, thinking him too old and too cautious. Fetterman had even boasted he could "ride through the Sioux Nation" with eighty men. That morning he received his opportunity when Carrington sent Fetterman and eighty men to provide relief to the wood train. Carrington authorized Fetterman to pursue the Lakota warriors as far as Lodge Trail Ridge but no farther. As Fetterman approached the skirmish, Crazy Horse played the decoy and fled, with the captain in hot pursuit. Against orders, Fetterman followed

Crazy Horse over Lodge Trail Ridge, out of sight of Fort Phil Kearny. There hundreds of Lakota, Cheyenne, and Arapaho warriors ambushed Fetterman and his soldiers. The ensuing Fetterman Fight, or Battle of the Hundred Slain, could be heard from the nearly finished fort, but by the time reinforcements arrived, Fetterman and all the soldiers and cavalry had been killed, stripped, and ritualistically mutilated.

Crazy Horse had inflicted the worst military defeat the U.S. Army had suffered on the Great Plains up to that time. Carrington sent news of the military disaster via a civilian messenger named John "Portugee" Phillips, who volunteered to carry the distress message to Fort Laramie with a request for reinforcements, new .50-caliber breech-loading Springfield single-shot rifles, and some seven-shot repeating Spencer carbines. Phillips chose one of Carrington's Kentucky Thoroughbreds, a horse named Dandy, and rode to Fort Reno. From there Phillips continued his 236-mile ride, arriving at Fort Laramie about 10 a.m. on Christmas Day.

In response to the defeat, the army relieved Carrington of his command and gave it to Brig. Gen. Henry W. Wessells, who arrived at Fort Phil Kearny on January 16, 1867. Wessells received wagonloads of supplies and the new Springfield rifles with enough center-fire cartridges to give fifty to every man. Meanwhile, the Lakotas and their allies, emboldened by their great victory over Fetterman, increased their resistance to the trail and its forts. On April 18 they killed John M. Bozeman. During a summer Sun Dance, they gathered spiritual and physical courage and decided to wipe out and destroy all the forts along the Bozeman Trail.

On August 1 one thousand to fifteen hundred Cheyenne and Arapaho warriors attacked a hay-cutting crew of twenty-one soldiers and nine civilians outside Fort C. F. Smith. The fort closed its gate and refused to send any reinforcements to the beleaguered band, who quickly constructed a log redoubt to fight behind. The men were armed with breech-loading Springfield Model 1866 rifles, which had a rate of fire of eight to ten shots per minute (in comparison, the muzzle-loading muskets fired three shots per minute) and could be reloaded while men were lying in a prone position. The Hayfield Fight raged from 9:30 a.m. to 5 p.m. The small band repelled repeated charges by warriors on horseback and on foot. Red Cloud's warriors tried to burn the men out, but their efforts failed. Of the thirty men, three were killed and four were wounded, while Indian casualty estimates range from eight to twenty-five killed and dozens more wounded.

The next day Red Cloud and Crazy Horse and one thousand Lakota warriors attacked a wagon box corral defended by twenty-six soldiers and six civilians. The Wagon Box Fight lasted from 7:30 a.m. until 1:30 p.m. The thirty-two Americans successfully held off hundreds of Lakota attackers, suffering six deaths. Lakota casualties numbered at least six killed and six wounded. Red Cloud and Crazy Horse learned that warriors armed with bows and arrows could not overwhelm soldiers armed with breech-loading rifles inside a fortification.

The following year representatives of the Lakota, Cheyenne, and Arapaho Nations again met at Fort Laramie with officials from the United States, drafting the 1868 Treaty of Fort Laramie. "From this day forward all war between the parties to this agreement shall forever cease," Article 1 of the treaty optimistically began. This treaty secured for the Sioux Nation the Black Hills, with the promise that no Americans would "ever be permitted to pass over, settle upon, or reside in" that territory. In return, Lakota leaders were required to turn over to U.S. officials any Indian who committed a depredation on anyone under the authority of the United States. Further, the

Fig. 20. *Red Cloud (1821–1909).* From John D. McDermott, *A Guide to the Indian Wars of the West* (Lincoln: University of Nebraska Press, 1998), 111.

Fig. 21. Gen. William Tecumseh Sherman. From Robert M. Utley, *Frontier Regulars* (Lincoln: University of Nebraska Press, 1984), 142.

Sioux agreed to "withdraw all opposition to the military posts or roads now established south of the North Platte River, or that may be established." The army abandoned the Bozeman Trail, the Lakotas burned down the forts, and tribes on the northern and central plains moved to reservations such as the Great Sioux Reservation in North and South Dakota.

After the Civil War, fighting shifted temporarily to the southern and central plains, where military outposts such as Fort McPherson, Nebraska, were now commanded by Civil War veterans. Heroes at places like Gettysburg and Chancellorsville, including Gen. William Tecumseh Sherman, Gen. Philip H. Sheridan, and Lt. Col. George Armstrong Custer, had been reassigned to the Great Plains. Reconstruction in the West meant the removal of Indigenous people from their ancestral homelands to reservations. The treaties signed at Medicine Lodge Creek, Kansas, in October 1867 relocated southern Plains Indian tribes such as the Kiowas, Comanches, Kiowa-Apaches, Southern Cheyennes, and Arapahos to reservations within Indian Territory.

New forts built adjacent to the reservations housed soldiers to oversee the distribution of provisions and provide supervision and enforcement. Fort Reno, in Indian Territory (present-day Oklahoma), for example, was constructed near the reservation of the southern Cheyenne and southern Arapaho Nations. From this fort, reservation-bound Indians received supplies and annuities, since they were not permitted to continue their traditional livelihoods.

Nevertheless, many Indigenous people did not like living within the confines of the reservation or the restrictions placed on their livelihoods. Some fled the reservation, hunted on the plains without permission, or raided surrounding communities in nearby Kansas. General Sheridan wanted to track down and punish tribal members who had raided settlements, taken captives, and fled south into Indian Territory. He instigated a strategy of winter campaigns to catch Indigenous families when they least expected it and were most vulnerable.

Fort Supply, in Indian Territory, was established in 1868 to supply soldiers engaged in winter campaigns. From Fort Supply, then called Camp Supply, Custer launched a surprise attack on Black Kettle's Cheyenne village on the Washita River in modern-day Oklahoma. On November 27 Custer's force of 574 soldiers attacked and killed between fifteen and seventy-five warriors and perhaps a dozen Cheyenne women and children. Of the 21 soldiers who died in the attack, 20 had been led by Joel Elliott, whom Custer failed to support; they were ambushed by warriors from other encampments as the troops pursued fleeing Indians. Following the attack, Custer hurried back to Camp Supply for refuge. The winter campaign worked, and the villages along the Washita returned to their reservations, where they lived in the shadows of a growing number of military forts.

In late 1875 the U.S. government issued an edict that all Lakotas needed to return to their reservations by January 1, 1876, or they would be considered hostile. As soon as spring came, Lakotas fled the reservations to join in the Sun Dance ceremony in the Rosebud River valley. On June 6 Hunkpapa Medicine Man and War Chief Sitting Bull offered one hundred pieces of flesh from his arms as a sacrifice and danced throughout the night until he fainted from the loss of blood. Sitting Bull regained consciousness and revealed a remarkable vision wherein he saw soldiers attack an Indian village, but they and their horses were upside down in the camp. The Lakotas interpreted this as meaning they would achieve a great victory.

Eleven days later, on June 17, the U.S. Army and their Crow and Shoshone allies fought against Lakotas and Northern Cheyennes at the Battle of the Rosebud. The Cheyennes call it the Battle Where the Girl Saved Her Brother because Buffalo Calf Road Woman protected her brother during the battle. The Lakotas and Cheyennes fought Gen. George Crook to a standstill, forcing Crook's army to retreat.

The conflict reached its climax a week later, on June 25, at the Battle of the Little Bighorn or Battle of the Greasy Grass. U.S. troops stationed at Fort Ellis (east of present-day Bozeman, Montana), Fort Fetterman (in present-day Wyoming), and Fort Abraham Lincoln (in present-day North Dakota), all constructed during the Indian Wars era, converged on an area suspected of being the site of a large encampment of Lakotas and their Cheyenne and Arapaho allies. Indeed, troops under Custer's command found, and were soon overwhelmed by, an estimated fifteen hundred to twenty-five hundred warriors. Over 270 soldiers, including Custer, perished. A week later, on July 4, 1876, the U.S. centennial celebration was marred by news of Custer's defeat and death. But the days of the Lakotas and other tribes living freely on the Great Plains came to an end as settlers staked out farms and ranches on formerly Indian-held lands and hide hunters slaughtered bison to near extinction.

The World Wars and After

With the conclusion of the Indian Wars era, some U.S. military forts were repurposed and played an important role in twentieth-century military objectives. For instance, as conflict between settlers and Indians subsided, Fort Clark, in southern Texas, was deemed unnecessary and threatened with closure. With the outbreak of the Mexican Revolution in 1912 and the ensuing turmoil along the Mexican-American border, however, the need to maintain Fort Clark became evident. It remained open during World War I and was used for training infantry and cavalry, a role that continued through the outbreak of World War II. With the development of new technologies, Fort Clark was one of the last military posts in the United States where horse cavalry were trained. German prisoners of war were also detained there during the war before Fort Clark was decommissioned in 1946.

Nebraska's Fort Robinson had started out as a U.S. military base during the Sioux wars of the 1870s. Lakota war chief Crazy Horse, who had achieved multiple victories over soldiers at the Fetterman Fight in 1866 and the Rosebud and the Little Bighorn battles in 1876, surrendered at Fort Robinson on May 6, 1877. Four months later, on September 5, a military guard killed him with a bayonet when the Oglala leader allegedly resisted imprisonment. In 1885 the African American Ninth Cavalry Regiment of Buffalo Soldiers was stationed there. During World War I the army repurposed the base to provide horses and mules as remounts to U.S. Army units. By 1919 it became the world's largest quartermaster remount depot. The Remount Service of the Quartermaster Corps at Fort Robinson instituted a breeding and training center for military horses and mules that remained in operation throughout World War II and continued until 1948, when all animal-breeding programs returned to the Department of Agriculture.

In the years following World War II, many other forts were closed. Between 1944 and 1949 Texas saw the closure of Fort Crockett, Fort McIntosh, Fort Ringgold, and Fort Travis. In Oklahoma, Fort Reno was deactivated in 1949. Nebraska saw the closure of Fort Omaha and Fort Robinson in 1947 and 1948, respectively. Across the Great Plains, forts that had been occupied for decades were deemed unneeded. Today many are state or national historic sites, some are private guest ranches, and others lay in ruins or have become ghost towns.

A handful of posts on the Great Plains continue to be used by the U.S. military into the twenty-first century. For example, Fort Leavenworth, Kansas, boasts of being the oldest active

Fig. 22. Fort Robinson stables. Wikimedia Commons.

military post west of the Mississippi River, having been repurposed to meet the changing needs of the U.S. Army. Those who first pitched their tents at Cantonment Leavenworth in 1827 would not recognize the sprawling 5,634-acre campus today, with over one thousand buildings and fifteen hundred quarters. Fort Leavenworth is the home of the U.S. Army Command and General Staff College, which offers graduate degrees for army officers. Dwight Eisenhower, George Patton, and tens of thousands of other officers have studied there. In addition, Fort Leavenworth houses a military correctional facility and includes a maximum-security prison. The Fort Leavenworth National Cemetery captures the historical and current importance of the site, with soldiers interred who served in the Mexican-American War, Civil War, Indian Wars, and every war of the twentieth century.

Fort Crook, Nebraska, is another active military post that was established in the nineteenth century. Within twenty-two years of when Fort Crook was built for the fight against Indians on the plains, it was being used to train pilots who operated reconnaissance balloons and flew airplanes in Europe during World War I. In 1924 Fort Crook was renamed Offutt Army Air Field in honor of a local pilot and veteran of World War

I, Jarvis Offutt. Over time, Offutt was used to train pilots in increasingly sophisticated planes. During World War II a manufacturing plant was housed at Offutt, building B-29 bombers. In 1947 the newly created U.S. Air Force gained control of the facility, renaming it Offutt Air Force Base. Offutt's location in the interior of the continent was viewed as a great asset, making it a difficult target for enemy attack. During the Cold War, Offutt was the site of the U.S. Strategic Air Command, operating long-range nuclear bombers out of range of enemy attack. With the easing of Cold War tensions, the Strategic Air Command was deactivated, though Offutt has maintained its prominent role in training members of the air force.

Several other military outposts still dot the Great Plains, each with a rich history and specialized significance. Fort Sill, Oklahoma, housed Apache prisoners of war, including Geronimo; Japanese American internees; and German prisoners of war during World War II. It has become the home of the U.S. Army Field Artillery School. Here pilots have trained on the Henry Post Army Airfield since 1917, and helicopter pilots have trained since the 1960s. One of the more recently constructed military outposts on the plains is Fort Carson, Colorado, established after the Japanese attack on Pearl Harbor. On the eastern fringe of the Rocky Mountains, Fort Carson provides a base from which soldiers can receive mountain warfare training and experience.

From the days of the Spanish presidios on the southern plains until the twenty-first century, military outposts have been constructed on the Great Plains. Their size, structure, and purposes have changed through the years, reflecting national interests and current needs. Some military outposts that once housed soldiers who protected emigrant trails now oversee missiles that could strike global targets. Others that were vital during the Indian Wars have long since been abandoned and now crumble in ruins. Several distant outposts have become thriving civilian communities, while others are remembered as historic sites. Military outposts of the plains have played a central role in shaping individual lives as well as the course of Indian nations and the United States.

Fig. 23. Canadian posts and forts. From James A. Hanson, *When Skins Were Money: A History of the Fur Trade* (Chadron NE: Museum of the Fur Trade, 2005), 168. Courtesy of James A. Hanson, Museum of the Fur Trade, Chadron NE.

CHAPTER FIVE

Canadian Prairies Posts

The Dominion of Canada, formed in 1867, united the eastern provinces of Nova Scotia, New Brunswick, Ontario, and Quebec into a single confederation independent of British colonial rule. One of the most significant events in its early years was the Red River Rebellion, an 1869 uprising against the government of Canada. Fort Garry, a trading post established by the Hudson's Bay Company (HBC) in 1822 on the confluence of the Red and Assiniboine Rivers south of Lake Winnipeg, played a central role in the unrest. During the early 1800s much of the Canadian Prairies had been under the influence of the HBC, which served as the de facto government of the region. By 1867, in addition to the First Nations who lived in the area, the land was home to thousands of Métis, the descendants of French trappers and Indigenous women. The French-speaking Métis lived, farmed, and engaged in trade within the Canadian Prairies. Some English-speaking trappers and settlers joined them, but the Métis and their Native neighbors remained an overwhelming majority of the population. The HBC acknowledged Métis and First Nations' right of occupancy without recognizing fee simple title ownership.

The Red River Rebellion occurred after the Canadian government purchased the prairies from the HBC and appointed an English-speaking governor, William McDougall, to administer

Fig. 24. *Fort Garry* (now Winnipeg, Manitoba). From H. J. Warre, *Sketches in North America and the Oregon Territory* (London, 1849). Courtesy Library and Archives Canada.

the territory. Fearing that the government of Canada might take their land and oppress the French speakers in the region, Louis Riel and many other Métis, together with some English allies, refused to allow McDougall to enter his jurisdiction. They seized and occupied Fort Garry, the symbolic capital of the territory, established their own provisional government, and began negotiations with Canadian officials. They demanded of the Canadian government fourteen guarantees that were intended to protect the rights of the Métis and their allies in the prairies.

Some English speakers supported Riel's movement, though a growing number favored Canadian rule. A group of Anglophones who supported Canadian sovereignty launched an assault on Fort Garry, determined to overthrow Riel's provisional government. Several of the counterrevolutionaries, including Thomas Scott, were taken prisoner after their unsuccessful

Fig. 25. Louis Riel. Courtesy Library and Archives Canada.

attempt to retake the fort. Scott's outspoken criticism of the
Métis' cause led the self-appointed provisional government to
try him for treason and insubordination. He was found guilty.
On March 4, 1870, Thomas Scott was executed by Riel's provisional government, shot by a firing squad against the wall of
Fort Garry, an incident with symbolic significance in the uprising. Most of the Métis's demands were ultimately met, and on
July 15 the province of Manitoba was created, with Fort Garry,
which grew into the city of Winnipeg, as its provincial capital.

The story of Fort Garry and other forts of the Canadian
Prairies is one of clashing cultures, struggles for self-rule, and

economic fortunes and misfortunes, with ambitious characters representing many backgrounds who overcame significant hardships. As was the case with the Great Plains of the United States, forts played an important role in the history of the Canadian Prairies, which stretches across the southern portions of Manitoba, Saskatchewan, and Alberta, collectively known as the Prairie Provinces.

Fort Garry rests on the eastern fringe of the prairie and, like many forts in the region, was built by the HBC to facilitate the fur trade. Even after the decline of beaver trapping, forts were used to promote trade in bison robes and other skins. Products moved freely along the rivers and trails that linked Canadian and U.S. forts. Eventually, forts were constructed by the North-West Mounted Police to subdue international trade in illicit products such as whiskey. From forts, Canadian officials brought law and order to the region, facilitated the construction of a transcontinental railroad, and oversaw the tragic subjugation of First Nations. Today the military bases on the Canadian Prairies maintain the international presence that was common in historic forts of the region.

The Early Fur Trade Era

Some of Canada's most important river systems cross the Canadian Prairies and include scores of tributaries. The relatively level topography of the prairies creates gentle rivers, arteries of trade that have been used for commerce for centuries. The Saskatchewan is the most important river system of the Canadian Prairies, though it is not the only drainage there.

ALONG THE SASKATCHEWAN RIVER AND TRIBUTARIES

The Saskatchewan River flows eastward from its tributaries in the Rocky Mountains, across the Canadian Prairies, to Lake Winnipeg on the prairies' eastern fringe. It meanders through the modern provinces of Alberta, Saskatchewan, and Manitoba. Although its name means "swift-flowing river" in the Indigenous Cree language, the Saskatchewan is navigable for most of its length and has been an important means of commerce for Indigenous peoples since before the arrival of European trappers and traders. French investors were extremely interested in entering the fur trade on the Saskatchewan. They built forts along the river, including Fort Bourbon at its mouth and Fort Paskoya near Cedar Lake, in present-day Manitoba. The westernmost post established by the French in their North American empire, Fort à la Corne, was built in 1752 near the confluence of the North and South Saskatchewan Rivers. Mixed evidence exists as to whether an additional proposed outpost, Fort La Jonquière, was constructed even farther west on the river's bank. If so, it did not operate for long. The 1763 fall of New France in the Seven Years' War caused the French to abandon their Canadian outposts, along with their claims to the territory.

Soon after France surrendered its North American empire, British fur companies, the HBC and its Montreal-based rival, the North West Company (NWC), established outposts on the Saskatchewan River, some of them near abandoned French forts. In 1774 the HBC reversed an earlier policy that had required Indigenous trappers to bring furs to company posts on Hudson's Bay. That year the HBC began to build depots in the interior to facilitate trade with it Indigenous partners. One of the most important HBC forts on the Canadian Prairies was Cumberland House, constructed in 1774 as company officials began to view inland forts as a means of expanding its reach. Over the next decades Cumberland House was used as a depot for storing furs to be shipped to the East and trade goods and pemmican to be conveyed to trappers in the West. In 1783 the fledgling NWC built a rival post near Cumberland House. Facing the challenge head-on, HBC relocated Cumberland House directly across the river from the NWC fort.

Increasing competition between the two companies in the 1790s caused both to build numerous forts along the Saskatchewan River and its north fork. The purpose of these forts was to facilitate trade with Indigenous trappers, increasing the likelihood of purchasing their pelts before the skins could be sold at a competitor's outpost. The rivalry between the NWC's Fort George and the HBC's Buckingham House is representative of this competition. In 1792 representatives of the NWC, frustrated by the declining numbers of beavers in lower stretches of the North Saskatchewan River, constructed Fort George about 120 miles upstream from the company's Pine Island Fort. Later that same year, employees of the HBC constructed Buckingham House just a few hundred yards away. Residents of these two outposts maintained a complex relationship. In 1794, when threatened by Indigenous people who were alarmed by the intrusion of Europeans into their homelands, residents of Buckingham House moved into Fort George for their mutual protection. When the threat subsided, their rivalry was renewed.

This same pattern of fort building continued until 1821, with forts being built, relocated, and abandoned according to changes in beaver populations and trends in trade. For instance, when the HBC constructed Fort Edmonton on the North Saskatchewan River in 1795 to be closer to beaver-rich waters, the NWC constructed Fort Augustus nearby. Between 1795 and 1885 the HBC built a series of forts named Fort Carlton on the North and South Saskatchewan Rivers. The first Fort Carlton was situated close to the abandoned French Fort à la Corne, near the confluence of the two rivers. The NWC soon established Fort St. Louis nearby. Both forts were eventually relocated to the South Saskatchewan River. Then in 1810 a new Fort Carlton was built at a ford on the North Saskatchewan. The NWC constructed Fort La Montée within the same stockade, later relocating the fort 3 miles upstream.

In 1821 the rivalry between the HBC and NWC came to an end. Under pressure from the British government, the two companies merged, keeping the name of the older and more established Hudson's Bay Company. For efficiency, some forts were abandoned, others were combined, and new forts were built at previously unoccupied locations. For example, after the merger, the NWC's Fort La Montée was dismantled and its resources floated downstream for use at Fort Carlton.

The HBC and NWC forts along the Saskatchewan Rivers served as important trade centers. Here Indigenous, Métis, and European trappers, traveling by canoe, exchanged beaver pelts for guns, traps, and other trade goods. Company officials used larger wooden York boats for bulkier shipments of pelts and supplies. Bulky bison robes could be transported overland via two-wheeled Red River carts drawn by oxen, horses, or mules. During winter months when the rivers froze over, forts were linked by trails traveled by horse-drawn sleds or dogsleds. In 1874 steamboats arrived on the Saskatchewan River, increasing the convenience of travel between forts and the fledgling agricultural settlements developing around some of them. Many of today's cities in Alberta and Saskatchewan have their origins in the forts built in the 1790s during the height of the rivalry between the HBC and NWC.

Interactions between the company officials and residents of the forts and members of the First Nations of the Canadian Prairies were usually friendly but at times could become violent. Most Indigenous people welcomed the construction of forts and outposts near their lands because of the opportunities it gave them to conveniently sell furs and procure guns, traps, and other supplies. As members of rival nations gained access to these new technologies, it became a matter of survival for others to obtain them as well. The HBC and NWC entered a land where alliances and rivalries had existed for generations, and First Nations peoples viewed these newcomers as potential allies. The fur companies exploited these rivalries and alliances to their benefit by establishing partnerships that promoted the fur trade. Unsurprisingly, at times the residents of the forts instigated or otherwise became entangled in violent conflicts.

One such incident occurred at the HBC's South Branch House in 1794. South Branch House was one of the few forts built on the South Saskatchewan River. Unlike the north fork, the south fork of the river passed through open prairie that was not ideal beaver country, so trappers paid it less attention. However, in 1785 both the HBC and NWC built forts on a big bend of the South Saskatchewan within a few hundred yards of each other. In 1794 more than one hundred warriors from the Gros Ventre Nation attacked South Branch House, killing the four company officials stationed there, along with the Indian men, women, and children who were present. Only one man escaped. The attackers moved on to the nearby NWC fort, but the residents there had enough advance warning to prepare for the assault and successfully defended the fort. Such large-scale attacks were rare, as First Nations generally welcomed or at least tolerated the presence of forts in their territory because of the opportunities forts provided for trade.

SOUTH OF THE SASKATCHEWAN DRAINAGE

The HBC built additional forts along other rivers to the south of the Saskatchewan. In 1824, just a few years after the merger, the officials of the new HBC began work on Fort Pelly at a strategic location on the Assiniboine River near where a relocated HBC fort, Fort Hibernia, had previously operated. Fort Pelly was placed at the southern terminus of a portage between the Swan and Assiniboine Rivers. Traders could transport furs by land from Fort Pelly to the Swan River, then by river to Lake Winnipeg, and from there to York Factory, the HBC's northern headquarters on Hudson's Bay. Additionally, goods brought into Fort Pelly could be shipped along the Assiniboine River to other outposts, including Fort Garry. Fort Pelly became the center of a trade network that included trappers working on the Red Deer, Swan, and Assiniboine Rivers, as well as their smaller tributaries. Land and river routes connected Fort Pelly with other outposts, such as a series of forts built by NWC and HBC representatives along the Qu'Appelle River, the most important of which was Fort Qu'Appelle.

In the early 1830s the threat of American expansion into the region led HBC officials to build a ring of outposts connected to Fort Pelly, including Manitoba House, Fort Ellice, the Touchwood Hills Post, Swan River House, Fort Swan Lake, and the Last Mountain Post. These posts were intended to make trade with Indigenous trappers more convenient and discourage them from taking their furs elsewhere for exchange. For instance, in 1831 HBC employees built Fort Ellice on Beaver Creek near the confluence of the Assiniboine and Qu'Appelle Rivers to secure trade with Cree and Assiniboine trappers who operated in that locality. Despite these new outposts, HBC trade suffered because of the higher prices American traders paid for furs, sometimes three times what their Canadian rivals offered. The challenge of competition with unaffiliated trappers continued into the 1850s and beyond. These "freemen," as they were sometimes called, were despised by trappers affiliated with the HBC or NWC. Freemen lived in Indigenous villages, traded for pelts harvested by Indian trappers, and delivered the skins to the company forts at prices higher than Native trappers received, thus cutting into the profits of the large fur companies.

One of the important roles of forts in this era was providing food for both the company employees and others who visited the posts to trade. Indigenous hunters often brought bison meat for exchange, sometimes in large quantities. An 1833 journal reported that Cree hunters had supplied 3,160 pounds of dried bison meat, 1,950 pounds of grease, and a small amount of bear meat to Fort Pelly. In addition, workers at forts sometimes established fisheries to meet the demand for food. These fisheries were often highly productive, with one in the Porcupine Hills processing two thousand to three thousand fish in a week and a half in 1835. Forts also became the sites of agriculture, with barley, wheat, and potatoes common crops produced in the brief Canadian growing season. Pests and late or early frost made farming a precarious pursuit. Ranching fared little better, as wolves and other predators threatened the horses, cattle, hogs, and hens that were raised at some forts. About 50 miles north of Fort Pelly, on the Swan River, workers used salt water collected at a spring to produce salt, a vital commodity that was useful for the preservation of meat and fetched a high price. Enterprises such as these allowed the forts to sell locally produced foodstuffs as well as the foods that were shipped there.

Although many outposts remained small and experienced only moderate and seasonal commercial activity, other forts became hubs of year-round trade and labor. Fort Pelly, for example, became an active community of exchange and manufacturing. Pit saws were employed to mill lumber into planks that could be used for the construction of boats, some of considerable size. One York boat made at Fort Pelly was 7.5 feet wide and 31 feet long. A blacksmith on site produced a variety of goods, including fish spears, nails, traps, and parts for gun repairs. Sleds, carts, and horse- and dog-drawn toboggans were also built at the fort. Trade goods were received at Fort Pelly to be shipped to its outposts for retail sale. Furs were brought into Fort Pelly from the surrounding outposts and were warehoused there until they could be shipped by sled or cart to Swan Lake.

In any given year a wide variety of furs besides beaver pelts made their way through Fort Pelly, including badger, otter, lynx, bear, and moose, as well as swan skins. When the spring thaws opened the water, company employees transported the furs that had been delivered to Swan Lake by boat to York Factory. Fort Pelly played such a central role in the commerce of the region that when fire destroyed its buildings in the winter of 1842–43, workers immediately began rebuilding them.

As was common with the forts that were hastily erected, in 1856 HBC officials determined that Fort Pelly should be moved to a new location, where its outlying resources would be less vulnerable to the seasonal flooding of the Assiniboine River. Accordingly, HBC workers constructed a new outpost about a quarter of a mile to the southeast. A year later construction on the new, spacious lodge continued, while the old fort remained of service to trappers and traders. The transition to the new Fort Pelly was gradual; two years after construction had been mainly completed, the old fort still housed men and livestock. A visitor in 1859 described the new fort: "Fort Pelly, pleasantly situated on rising ground, is a new, square, white-washed cottage with small dormer windows in the roof, and offers better accommodation than any house I have seen since leaving Red River. Various outhouses for stores, etc, surround it at the back and sides, but the Saulteaux Indians of the district are so peaceable that no stockade has been thought necessary." The new fort attracted visitors for holiday celebrations, with feasts followed by games of "football" and dancing. Religious missionaries in the area conducted church services at Fort Pelly, sometimes administering communion in the language of Indigenous worshippers.

After 1870, when HBC surrendered its control of the territory to the Canadian government, Fort Pelly declined in importance. The management of the region was shifted to Fort Ellice to the south. Within a decade railroads and steamboats were changing the cycles of trade that had made Fort Pelly so important within the region. The history of Fort Pelly is representative of the forts established in the southern Canadian Prairies.

A New Fort-Building Era

Trappers for the HBC and NWC had been using the rivers of the Canadian Prairies as pathways of commerce, loading canoes with beaver furs and other skins and transporting them along streams and rivers. With the decline of the beaver trade in the 1840s, however, new commodities gained importance, some of which were difficult to ship in canoes. Bison, harvested primarily for their thick hides, became one of the most exploited resources of the Great Plains and Canadian Prairies at about the same time that the beaver trade went into decline. But large quantities of bison robes, the term for skins with the hair left in place, were difficult to transport by canoe, leading to changing dynamics in prairie trade.

Political transformations contributed to changing patterns in trade as well. When the Dominion of Canada purchased control of the vast lands in western Canada from the HBC in 1869, the Canadian government was ill prepared to police the immense region. The vacuum created by the exit of the HBC provided an opportunity for ambitious entrepreneurs to engage in lucrative trade in buffalo robes and other commodities, including whiskey, the trading of which had become illegal in Montana that same year.

John J. Healy and Alfred B. Hamilton were two of the first businessmen to take advantage of this opportunity. Recognizing the proximity of Fort Benton on the Upper Missouri River to the vast Canadian Prairies, and appreciating the relative ease of wagon travel across the gentle plains, the duo devised a plan. They could ship trade goods of value to Métis, Blackfoot, and other Indigenous hunters and trappers by steamboat to Fort Benton. From there, the goods could be loaded into wagons and taken north, crossing the Canadian border. In Canada, these trade goods could be exchanged for buffalo robes and other skins and furs, which could be hauled back to Fort Benton and then shipped by steamboat for processing.

In 1869 Healy and Hamilton put their plan into action. Orders of rifles, ammunition, blankets, tobacco, sugar, knives, beads, and whiskey arrived at Fort Benton. The partners and their employees loaded the goods into wagons and carted them into Blackfoot territory. As they traveled north, they exchanged goods for robes and skins as planned. At the confluence of the St. Mary's and Belly Rivers, near the location of modern Lethbridge, Healy and Hamilton hastily constructed a fort, Fort Hamilton, where they spent about six months exchanging trade goods for buffalo robes. They returned the 200 miles to Fort Benton in wagons loaded with about $50,000 worth of robes and furs, a relative fortune. They made plans to go back to the Canadian Prairies the following year, even after fire destroyed Fort Hamilton.

The next year they returned with a crew of workers, who spent two years constructing a heavily defended fort. Conflict between the Blackfeet Confederacy nations and the Assiniboines and their allies placed traders' lives in jeopardy. Workers prepared the new Fort Hamilton for a direct attack, with a stockade, bastions with mounted cannons, and protected areas from which to fire rifles. From Fort Hamilton, the lucrative trade continued, with whiskey becoming the most valuable commodity. John Healy's stepson later remembered how the whiskey flowed at the fort: "The trader stood at a wicket, a tub full of whiskey beside him, and when an Indian pushed a buffalo robe to him through the hole, he handed out a tin cup full of the poisonous decoction [whiskey]. A quart of the stuff bought a fine pony."

One of the traders, after returning to Fort Benton, was asked how things were going at Fort Hamilton. He replied that they were still "a whoopin' 'er up." People were soon referring to Fort Hamilton as Fort Whoop-Up, and the trade route to the fort became known as the Whoop-Up Trail. Travelers could reach Fort Whoop-Up from Fort Benton in about eight days by following the trail.

It was not long before other traders became engaged in the highly profitable traffic of buffalo robes and whiskey. But by the 1870s the bison population of the Canadian Prairies had declined significantly. In response, some hunters began to specialize in "wolfing," hunting, trapping, or poisoning wolves to harvest their pelts. Two wolf pelts were similar in value to a single buffalo robe, and the practice of wolfing reenergized the ongoing trade along the Whoop-Up Trail.

Between 1869 and 1875 American and Canadian entrepreneurs constructed forty-five "whiskey posts" along the Whoop-Up Trail, some of them surviving only a season and others becoming more permanent outposts. Among the most notable was Fort Kipp, built in 1871 at the junction of the Belly and Old Man Rivers by Joseph Kipp and partner Charles Thomas. Kipp and Thomas viewed the heavy defenses of Fort Whoop-Up as unnecessary and instead built a three-walled structure with an open fourth side that faced the river. From Fort Kipp, the team carried on a lucrative trade for several years, making the annual journey to Fort Benton to deliver robes and restock trade goods. Other forts along the Whoop-Up Trail included Berry's and Shear's Fort, Bonds Fort, Neil Campbell's Fort, Hand Hills Fort, Fort Conrad, Fort Shaw, Fort Standoff, Fort Thomas, Fort Warren, and Fort Weatherwax. The precise locations of some of these small outposts built on both sides of the Canadian-U.S. border remain unknown. White, Métis, American Indian, and African American traders all participated

Fig. 26. Fort Whoop-Up, ca. 1874. Courtesy Library and Archives Canada.

in the trade along the Whoop-Up Trail. Traffickers crossed the international border with little interference from the government of either nation until 1875.

A Turning Point on the Canadian Plains

The year 1873 marked a turning point in trade along the Whoop-Up Trail and in fort building in the western prairies of Canada. In May of that year a group of American and Canadian traders and wolfers crossed the border from Fort Benton into Canada to attempt to retrieve horses they believed had been stolen by Assiniboine raiders. On June 1 a confrontation between the makeshift posse and the residents of an Assiniboine village at Cypress Hills escalated into a massacre. Thirteen or more Assiniboines were killed, along with one French Canadian trapper who had attacked the village with the intoxicated posse.

When news of the Cypress Hills Massacre reached Canadian officials, they decided that something had to be done about the lawlessness of the region, and a new period of fort building

Fig. 27. Whoop-Up trail caravan. Wikimedia Commons.

began. The North-West Mounted Police (NWMP), who arrived on the Canadian Prairies in 1874, constructed forts to facilitate the enforcement of an 1867 law that made trade in whiskey illegal. These forts and the presence of the NWMP reaffirmed Canada's control of the region and dispelled any thought that individuals in the United States might have had about increasing the U.S. influence there. Rather than ending the cross-border trade, the presence of the NWMP increased trade between Fort Benton, the Canadian forts the police manned, and the settlements that grew around those forts.

In 1874, during what is referred to as the Great March West, 275 men of the NWMP left Fort Dufferin on the eastern fringe of the Canadian Prairie, determined to drive out whiskey traders from the United States and bring law and order to the Canadian West. However, without an established east-west land route, crossing the prairie proved to be more challenging than expected. Water was often difficult to locate, and the dry conditions weakened livestock and delayed travel. Winter arrived as

Fig. 28. Fort Whoop-Up National Historic Site. Wikimedia Commons.

the troops neared Fort Whoop-Up. Unaware of their proximity to the fort, the troops prepared to make a winter camp on the open plains as the first snows fell in September. Splitting into three groups, some remained at the winter encampment, while others returned east to Fort Pelly, the well-established HBC post on the Assiniboine River. The third contingent turned south toward Fort Benton to secure much-needed supplies. American traders at Fort Whoop-Up, who were tipped off that the NWMP had been dispatched, abandoned the outpost before those at the winter encampment eventually found their way there. In October the police force went to work constructing a new fort, Fort Macleod.

In the years following the arrival of the NWMP, Fort Macleod quickly grew into a thriving outpost, with police barracks, hospital, stores, stables, and a blacksmith shop. The fort became the headquarters of the NWMP in 1876, two years after its construction. Whiskey peddlers who wished to continue their illicit operations were pushed to new locations. As the smugglers relocated, officials of the NWMP built additional forts in order to patrol the vast prairies. In 1875 work began on Fort Calgary at the confluence of the Bow and Elbow Rivers, the midpoint between Fort Macleod and Fort Edmonton. Like Fort Macleod, Fort Calgary attracted a variety of business interests. The HBC relocated its Ghost River trading post to Calgary. A private trading post and storehouse were also built nearby. A Catholic mission was briefly housed at the fort.

As occurred with many of the forts throughout the Canadian Prairies, a town developed near Fort Macleod and Fort Calgary. In the early 1900s Fort Macleod assumed a new role as a divisional point of the Canadian Pacific Railway, increasing the European population of the town that was expanding around the fort. Fort Calgary, too, grew after 1882 when it became an NWMP district post.

One of the challenges in studying the forts of the Canadian Prairies and elsewhere is the then common practice of renaming and relocating forts. For instance, Fort Calgary was originally named the Bow River Fort until the commander who oversaw its construction decided to rename it after himself, Fort Brisebois. Officials of the NWMP were unimpressed by Brisebois's leadership or name selection and settled on a new name, Fort Calgary, after a Scottish castle on the Isle of Mull. Additionally, forts of this and earlier eras were often hastily constructed, with the later realization that their placement was less than ideal. Seasonally flooding rivers, newly perceived vulnerabilities, and the discovery of superior sites led to the relocation of forts, sometimes only a stone's throw from their original plot and other times miles away. Fort Macleod, for example, was rebuilt in 1884 at an entirely new spot. It was not only the NWMP forts that had such complex histories; the earlier fur-trapping outposts went through similar transitions.

The NWMP built forts with the intention of ending the influence of traders from south of the border; however, the strategy was only partially successful. Though the police curbed the whiskey trade in the region, the developing communities around the forts created a new market for American goods, expanding the Fort Benton trade. The law and order established by the NWMP attracted new settlers into the region, increasing the demand for trade goods produced in the United States. The illicit whiskey trade was replaced by the exchange of more respectable commodities, a market that enriched merchants from south of the border. Nevertheless, the presence of the NWMP successfully eliminated threats of political U.S. encroachment into the Prairie Provinces but not U.S. commercial influence.

The North-West Rebellion and Aftermath

This chapter opened with the story of Fort Garry and the 1869 Red River Rebellion, led by Louis Riel. In the years after that relatively successful rebellion, new settlers poured into the region, pushing out many of the Red River Métis. Riel left Manitoba and relocated to Fort Benton in Montana, becoming a moderately successful trader and schoolteacher and a natu-ralized U.S. citizen. In the meantime, trouble was brewing in Saskatchewan. By 1885 the increasing scarcity of bison caused unrest among the First Nations, and the survival-driven transi-tion from hunting to agriculture presented challenges for Métis families, not the least of which were issues over landownership. New Anglophone settlers in the area were likewise frustrated by the unresponsive Canadian government. Seeking a charismatic leader who could unite these disparate voices, the settlers sent a delegation to Fort Benton to persuade Riel to return to Canada to lead the demand for reform.

Riel obliged and returned to the Canadian Prairies to lead a new fight for rights. He originally assumed a moderate stance that attracted the interests of First Nations, Métis, and Anglo settlers in Saskatchewan. However, his religious zeal led him to adopt views that were considered heretical, and he lost the support of church leaders and their congregations. His political stance gradually became more extreme as well, losing him the support of Anglo settlers. Eventually, only a small group of Métis and a handful of Indigenous people supported his North-West Rebellion. Still, the rebels established the Provisional Government of Saskatchewan, replacing, in their minds, the existing inept government of the province.

The first shots of the North-West Rebellion were fired near Fort Carlton, when a party of Métis discovered and massacred a small contingency of police from the fort. Fort Carlton was soon abandoned by the NWMP and occupied by the rebel forces. The revolution's success at Fort Carlton proved to be short-lived, however, as Canadian forces from the East were quickly transported by railroad to crush the rebellion. Riel was captured and tried for treason. Disputes arose about whether he should be tried in Winnipeg, near the site of Fort Garry, where Riel first rose to prominence, or in Regina, a community that lacked the long history and diversity of communities that had originated as French or fur company forts. Government officials determined that Regina would be the better location, and an all-Anglo jury was selected. Riel was convicted, though the jurors requested that the judge grant him leniency. Judge Hugh Richardson accepted the guilty verdict but rejected the jurors' plea for leniency, citing the decision of Riel's provision government to slay Thomas Scott during the Red River Rebellion sixteen years earlier as grounds for his execution. Riel was hanged on November 16, 1885, at the NWMP barracks in Regina. Riel's trial and execution were symbolic of other changes, as settlers brought an increasing Anglo presence and the NWMP brought a new system of law and order that ushered in the twentieth century.

Modern Military Bases on the Canadian Prairies

Today the Canadian Army operates several army and air force bases on the prairies, each of which has maintained the international flair that characterized the frontier forts. For example, in the province of Alberta, Canadian Forces Base Edmonton rests on the outskirts of the community that grew around the HBC's 1795 Fort Edmonton. From this airfield, which was expanded with U.S. support during World War II, Canadian pilots trained, and U.S. pilots moved supplies and troops into Alaska. Ground forces stationed at the base conducted exercises in survival during harsh Alberta winters. Southeast of Edmonton near the city of Suffield, Canadian Forces Base Suffield claims to be the largest military training facility in Canada. The region's harsh and dry landscape was of little use for agriculture or other economic pursuits, so in 1941 Canadian officials purchased land owned by the HBC and by the Canadian Pacific Railway for experimentation with chemical weapons and other training purposes. This facility has been used in cooperation with the British military since World War II and continues to be operated in coordination with the British. The Canadian Air Force Base at Moose Jaw, Saskatchewan, has been used to train pilots from Belgium, Czechoslovakia, France, the Netherlands, New Zealand, Norway, the United Kingdom, and the United States. Though the number of forts on the Canadian Prairies has decreased dramatically with the dawn of the twentieth century, their size and international importance have grown.

Forts have played a significant role in the exploration, exploitation, and settlement of the Canadian Prairies. From the early forts built during the years of France's North American empire and at the height of the Hudson's Bay and North West Companies' competition in the fur trade to those constructed by

U.S. whiskey purveyors and the NWMP, forts have shaped and been shaped by the history of the prairies. Forts have been of importance to the economic success and ultimate decimation of First Nations. They have been cultural melting pots where French, British, American, Métis, and Indigenous people have collaborated and competed. They have been built, relocated, renamed, abandoned, and in some cases reclaimed by the Canadian Prairies to the extent that their original locations often cannot be identified. A number of forts have grown into some of the largest communities of the region, including Winnipeg, Calgary, Edmonton, and Prince Albert. Today military outposts continue to have an economic impact on the communities where they operate, bringing in international guests. Natives, Métis, Canadians, and Europeans who interacted with these forts played a significant role in the history of the Canadian Prairies.

SITE GUIDE

This guide includes alphabetical listings by province or state of forts built on the Canadian Prairies and the U.S. Great Plains, or along the borderlands, as well as Indigenous fortifications in these regions. These lists are simplified, as sometimes forts went by various names during their years of operation or the same name was applied to multiple outposts constructed near the same location at different times. The locations of many Native fortifications are withheld from public knowledge to protect the delicate and sacred artifacts and human remains there; only those that are protected as national or state historic sites are listed.

Indigenous Fortifications

Fort	Years of operation	Description
Alcova Redoubt Site	ca. 400–1200 AD	Fortified prehistoric site (48NA3502) that contains a 723-foot wall with bastions and weapons systems. West of Alcova Reservoir in the northern Platte River basin in Wyoming.
Crow Creek National Historic Landmark	ca. 1300s AD	Represents a significant prehistoric Native massacre of nearly 500 men, women, and children by another Indigenous group ca. 1325. Near Chamberlain, Buffalo County, South Dakota.
Grapevine Creek Battle Site	ca. 1850s AD	Consists of 23 defensive bulwarks in a circle on top of a bluff. Built by 35 Piegan Blackfeet raiders who were defeated by Stump Horn and other Crow warriors in battle. On the Crow Reservation 8 miles southwest of Fort Smith, Montana.
Knife River Indian Villages National Historic Site	ca. 1600s AD	Site established in 1974 that preserves the historic and archaeological remnants of Hidatsas. Consists of three Hidatsa villages—Awatixa Xi'e (lower Hidatsa), Awatixa, and Big Hidatsa—lining the banks of the confluence of the Knife and Missouri Rivers. Half a mile north of Stanton, North Dakota, and one hour northwest of Bismarck.

| Molander Indian Village State Historic Site | ca. 1700s AD | Home to the Awaxawi Hidatsa around 1764, with nearly 40 houses that each held an extended family of up to 20 people, as well as a fortification ditch, wooden palisades, and 6 bastions, uncovered by archaeologists in 1968. Overlooks the Missouri River 20 miles north of Mandan, North Dakota. |
| Writing-on-Stone Provincial Park | ca. 7000 BC–1957 AD | Sacred site known to the Blackfoot as Áísínai'pi (meaning "it is pictured"). Has the greatest concentration of rock art on the Great Plains and Canadian Prairies. Now a national historic site along the Milk River 60 miles southeast of Lethbridge, Alberta, Canada. |

Forts on the Canadian Prairies

ALBERTA

The northwest region of the Great Plains extends into Alberta, Canada. Here the Hudson's Bay Company and its rival, the North West Company, built trading posts as early as the 1790s. By the 1870s forts were established by the Canadian government to house the North-West Mounted Police (NWMP), protect settlers, reinforce Canada's claim to the territory, put down insurrection, and establish a police presence in the thinly settled region. Alberta's most colorful outpost may have been Fort Hamilton, nicknamed Fort Whoop-Up, built by American businessmen who saw a market for smuggled liquor. Since the dawn of the twentieth century a limited number of Canadian Forces bases (CFBs) have been built on the Canadian Prairies to support national defense.

Fort	Years of operation	Description
Fort Augustus	1794–1821	Built by the North West Company near present-day Edmonton to facilitate the fur trade on the Saskatchewan River. Merged with Fort Edmonton in 1821.
Fort Calgary	1875–1914	Police fort built as NWMP Fort Brisebois in present-day Calgary. Became an NWMP district headquarters and eventually grew into the city of Calgary. Located at Fort Calgary Historic Park in Calgary.
CFB Calgary	1910 and 1933–97	Originally Harvey Barracks (1910), used to train troops during World War I, and Currie Barracks (1933), used to train infantry and air force, both in Calgary. Combined and continued to serve as a site to train troops until 1997 closure.
CFB Cold Lake	1954–present	Air force base constructed in Cold Lake during the height of the Cold War. Used in missile testing with the United States and in NATO training.
Fort Edmonton	1795–1915	Established by the Hudson's Bay Company as a fortified trading post in present-day Edmonton. Merged with rival Fort Augustus in 1821, becoming a hub of fur trade. Periodically rebuilt until dismantled in 1915. Located at Fort Edmonton Park in Edmonton.

CFB Edmonton	1941–present	Private airfield near Edmonton that became a training base for the Royal Canadian Air Force and its allies during World War II. Became CFB Edmonton, used primarily for training ground forces.
Fort Macleod	ca. 1874–94	First permanent NWMP fort in the British Northwest. Established to protect Canadian land claims and combat the illegal whiskey trade. Evolved into the town of Fort Macleod by 1894, which today contains Fort Macleod National Historic Site of Canada.
Fort Normandeau	ca. 1885–93	Constructed near present-day Red Deer during the Northwest Rebellion to quell an uprising by Métis, Assiniboine, and Cree fighters. Occupied by the NWMP during the rebellion and later used as a base to monitor the district. The reconstructed Fort Normandeau is west of Red Deer.
Fort Saskatchewan	1875–1904	NWMP fort established in response to the need for law enforcement in the region. Eventually expanded into the town that still bears its name, which today contains Fort Saskatchewan Museum and Historic Site.
CFB Suffield	1941–present	Canada's largest military training area, near Ralston, originally created during World War II on mostly unoccupied land and used for training and to test chemical weapons. Used today to train British and Canadian forces.

CFB Wainwright	1940–present	Used in infantry and live-fire artillery training and as a prisoner-of-war camp during World War II and after. Downsized in the 1990s but continues in operation today in Denwood.
Fort Whoop-Up (Fort Hamilton)	1869–74	Founded near Lethbridge by American businessmen to capitalize on trade in bison robes and illicit whiskey. Abandoned when the NWMP entered the region in 1874. Fort Whoop-Up National Historic Site of Canada is in Lethbridge.

Manitoba, stretching from the eastern Great Plains to Hudson Bay, was the scene of extensive HBC and NWC fur trade operations. Starting in the 1730s several forts were constructed on the northeastern fringe of the Canadian Prairies by the HBC to facilitate trade with Natives. Later, HBC and NWC forts helped secure British and Canadian land claims, became an operational base for the North-West Mounted Police (NWMP), and served as launching sites from which to increase governmental authority in the region.

Fort	Years of operation	Description
Fort Dauphin	ca. 1741–1759	French fur trading post destroyed by First Nations soon after its establishment and rebuilt around 1743. Replica of the palisaded post is in present-day Dauphin.
Fort Douglas	1812–26	Constructed as a fur-trading post by the Hudson's Bay Company. Later housed the governor of the settlement until destroyed by a flood in 1826. Historic site marker is in Fort Douglas Park, Winnipeg.
Fort Dufferin	1872–79	Served as base of operations for the North American Boundary Commission and later as Manitoba's southern border immigration station. Also used as a base by the NWMP. Fort Dufferin National Historic Site of Canada is near Emerson.
Fort Ellice	ca. 1831–70	Hudson's Bay Company fur-trading post built on the Qu'Appelle River in 1831. Protected claims to the company's land and sold provisions, tools, and traps to passing traders. Fort Ellice interpretive center is in St. Lazare, and a historic site marker is nearby.
Fort des Epinettes	ca. 1784–94	Fur-trading post of the North West Company on the Assiniboine River, established as a center of trade with the Mandans and a supply post. Historic site marker is at Kiche Manitou Campground, Spruce Woods Provincial Park.

Lower Fort Garry	1830–1911	Built in 1830 by the Hudson's Bay Company as a trading post on the Red River. Site of an important treaty between seven First Nations and Canada. Lower Fort Garry National Historic Site of Canada is near Winnipeg.
Upper Fort Garry	ca. 1822–88	Replaced Fort Gibraltar in 1822 and served as the center of trade for the Red River settlement. Played a key role in the Red River Rebellion and the founding of Manitoba, eventually growing into the city of Winnipeg. Upper Fort Garry Provincial Park on the site of the original fort is in downtown Winnipeg.
Fort Gibraltar	1810–22	Fur-trading post constructed by the North West Company near rival Fort Douglas of the Hudson's Bay Company. Renamed (Upper) Fort Garry in 1822 after the two companies merged. Fort Gibraltar rebuilt in 1978 in St. Boniface, across the river from its original site.
Fort La Reine	ca. 1738–52	A series of early French fur-trading posts along the Assiniboine River. Original fort used as launch site for early expeditions that crossed the Canadian Prairies to the Rocky Mountains. Historic site marker and Fort La Reine Museum are in Portage la Prairie.

Fort Montagne à la Bosse	ca. 1790–1805	Trading post of the North West Company that served as a meat depot, providing pemmican and meat to boat crews on the Assiniboine River who transported furs from the West. Historic site marker is in the rural municipality of Wallace-Woodworth.
Fort Paskoya	1740–59	French fur trade–era fort built on the Saskatchewan River near Cedar Lake before the fall of New France. Site museum is in The Pas.
Fort Rouge	1738–49 1752–53	Early French trading post built by French trapper Pierre Gaultier de Varennes et de La Vérendrye. Abandoned around 1749. Briefly reoccupied by Jacques Legardeur de Saint-Pierre in the winter of 1752–53. Forts Rouge, Garry, and Gibraltar National Historic Site of Canada is in Winnipeg.
CFB Shilo	1910–present	Training facility east of Brandon, used for artillery and munitions training during World War I, parachute training during World War II, and international training since the 1970s.
CFB Winnipeg	1922–present	Air force base near Winnipeg established after World War I. Role in training grew during World War II. Continues to be used in training air force pilots and navigators.

SASKATCHEWAN

Between Alberta and Manitoba, Saskatchewan lies at the heart of the Canadian Prairies. Throughout the 1700s French and British fur companies competed for economic control of the region, using trading posts as a means of building alliances with local First Nations. Later, forts were used to house the North-West Mounted Police (NWMP) and discourage American encroachment on Canadian territory. Several of the forts grew into the cities and towns that dot Saskatchewan today.

Fort	Years of operation	Description
Fort Alexandria	ca. 1780–1821	Two trading posts of the North West Company, the first built on the Assiniboine River and then relocated in 1805 to the Fraser River. Abandoned when the North West and Hudson's Bay Companies merged. Fort Alexandria National Historic Site of Canada is in Alexandria.
Fort Battleford	1876–85	NWMP fort built by Canadian officials that served as the first seat of government in the Northwest Territories. The fort is preserved at Fort Battleford National Historic Site of Canada in Battleford.
Fort Carlton	1810–85	Hudson's Bay Company trading post established as the company expanded operations inland. Rivaled the North West Company's outposts and was a transportation hub and distributor of pemmican. Partially reconstructed fort is in Fort Carlton Provincial Park in Duck Lake.
Fort à la Corne	ca. 1753–1932	Westernmost French fort in Canada, built on the Saskatchewan River but closed when New France fell in 1763. Site reoccupied by a North West Company fort. Fort à la Corne National Historic Site of Canada historic marker is in Prince Albert.
Fort Esperance (Fort Qu'-Appelle)	ca. 1787–1819	Important trading post of the North West Company and the main pemmican depot in the company's continental fur trade. A distinct Hudson's Bay outpost shared the Qu'Appelle name. Historic site marker for Fort Esperance National Historic Site of Canada is in Rocanville.

Fort Livingston	1874–84	Fort constructed by Canadian officials as the first headquarters for the NWMP due to the need for a police presence. Historic site marker for Fort Livingston National Historic Site of Canada is in Pelly.
CFB Moose Jaw	1941–present	Used as an air force base and in pilot training since 1941, training pilots from across Europe and North America. South of Moose Jaw.
Fort Pelly	1856–1912	Headquarters of the Swan River District of the Hudson's Bay Company, serving outlets along the Assiniboine and Swan Rivers. Historic site marker is at Fort Pelly National Historic Site of Canada near Pelly.
Fort Pitt	1830–90	Major trading post of the Hudson's Bay Company, built on one of the main overland routes to Canada's interior. Served as a provisioning post and transportation hub. Historic site marker and remains of Fort Pitt National Historic Site of Canada are in Fort Pitt Provincial Park near Hewitt Landing.
Fort Walsh	ca. 1875–81	Military fort intended to curb the illegal whiskey trade, protect Canada's nearby border with the United States, and maintain peace with local First Nations. Reconstructed fort is at Fort Walsh National Historic Site of Canada, in Cypress Hills Interprovincial Park southwest of Maple Creek.

Forts on the Great Plains

In Colorado, the Great Plains meet the Rocky Mountains. This important geographic transition created a need for trappers, traders, settlers, and soldiers to resupply and reoutfit, resulting in the construction of several forts. Additionally, Colorado is at an important political crossroads, having been controlled by some of the most powerful Native nations even as Spain, the United States, and Mexico claimed the land by right of discovery. Forts were constructed to facilitate trade, monitor Indigenous groups, and strengthen claims to the territory. They were important landmarks on the Santa Fe Trail and other transportation routes across the Great Plains of Colorado, providing supplies and a welcome respite from the journey. Forts later housed soldiers assigned to push Natives onto reservations. Fort Carson, built in the twentieth century, continues to operate as an important military base.

Fort	Years of operation	Description
Old Bent's Fort	1833–49	Privately constructed trading post that became an important and prosperous trading center and rendezvous point for traders and Indigenous people along the Santa Fe Trail. Bent's Old Fort National Historic Site is near La Junta.
New Bent's Fort	1853–60	New fort built near present-day Lamar to replace Old Bent's Fort. Operated for over a decade bur did not experience the success of its predecessor. Purchased by the U.S. military in 1860 to use as storage for nearby Fort Lyon.
Fort Carson	1942–present	Military fort built during World War II. Housed Axis prisoners of war and is still in operation as a U.S. Army base south of Colorado Springs.
Fort Collins	ca. 1864–67	Military fort established during the Civil War to protect the Cherokee Trail and Overland Stage Line. Grew into the town of Fort Collins. Original fort site is now adjacent to the historic Old Town portion of the city of Fort Collins.
Fort Garland	1858–83	Military fort built to replace Fort Massachusetts. Protected the region's settlers and was active during the Civil War and Indian Wars. Fort Garland is home to Fort Garland Museum and Cultural Center.

Fort Jackson	1837–38	Fur trading post built near present-day Plattesville, strategically near the wintering grounds of the Cheyennes and Arapahos. Short-lived but profitable post.
Fort Junction	ca. 1864	Built by a local militia, the Vrain Valley Home Guards, as a refuge for settlers after a family was massacred during Indigenous unrest. Historic site marker is near Firestone.
Fort Logan	1887–1946	Military fort created in response to prominent Denver citizens who requested increased protection. Boosted the local economy and facilitated the use of railroads to transport troops and supplies.
Fort Lupton (Fort Lancaster)	ca. 1836–45, 1859–64	Private trading post built during the waning years of the fur trade. Abandoned in 1845 and reoccupied from 1859 to 1864 by a variety of groups. A re-creation of Lupton's Fort is located at South Platte Valley Historic Park near present-day Fort Lupton.
Fort Lyon (Fort Wise)	1860–67	Originally known as Fort Wise, a military fort protecting emigrants on the Santa Fe Trail. Important during the wars against Southern Cheyennes and Arapahos, especially the Sand Creek Massacre of 1864. Historic marker is west of Lamar.

Fort Lyon II	1867–89, 1906–22	Military fort established near Las Animas to replace the original Fort Lyon. Closed in 1889 but reoccupied in 1906 by the U.S. Navy for use as a tuberculosis hospital until 1922. Site includes Colorado National Cemetery and Kit Carson Memorial Chapel. Historic marker is near Wiley.
Fort Massachusetts	1852–58	Military fort established to protect settlers of the San Luis Valley and guard the Sangre de Cristo Pass. Vulnerable location and unhealthy swampy environment led to abandonment. Model of fort is on display at nearby Fort Garland Museum in Fort Garland.
Fort Morgan	1865–68	Military post just north of present-day Fort Morgan that protected the overland mail route from Indigenous raids. The only army presence between central Colorado and the populated regions of the Rocky Mountains.
Fort Pueblo	1842–54	Established by independent traders near present-day Pueblo to facilitate trade with Ute and Apache Indians. Thrived for more than a decade but was abandoned after Utes attacked the fort in 1854.
Fort Reynolds	1867–72	Military post established to supply Fort Lyon during the Indian Wars and to police nearby settlements. Historic marker is 1 mile east of present-day Avondale.

Fort Sedgwick	1864–71	Military fort founded during Native uprisings in the summer of 1864. Protected settlers, emigrants, and the transportation routes to Denver. Historic marker is in Ovid, and Fort Sedgwick Museum is in nearby Julesburg.
Fort St. Vrain	1837–38	Short-lived trading post on the Platte River during the waning years of the fur trade, built and operated by Bent, St. Vrain & Company, a fur-trading business. Historic marker near Platteville indicates the site of the fort.
Fort Vasquez	1835–42	Fur-trading post strategically located between Fort Laramie, Wyoming, and Bent's Old Fort. Promoted trade with the Cheyenne and Arapaho Nations. Fort Vasquez restoration and museum are near Platteville.
Spanish Fort (name unknown)	1819–21	Spanish military post established in present-day Costilla and Huerfano Counties and Spain's settlement to guard the Sangre de Cristo Pass against possible U.S. invasion of New Mexico.

Kansas

Kansas lies at the heart of the Great Plains and the geographic center of the United States. Early forts built in Kansas outfitted and protected travelers along the Santa Fe Trail and other transportation routes. Conflicts escalated between Indigenous peoples who had lived on the land for centuries and new arrivals, which included emigrant Natives and Euro-American settlers. As violence increased, so did the number of military outposts. Forts in Kansas fell into two categories: those designed to protect overland travelers and newly arrived settlers and military installations constructed after the Civil War during the Indian wars. The military abandoned most Kansas forts after Native nations relocated to reservations.

Fort	Years of operation	Description
Fort Atkinson	1850–54	Military fort on the Arkansas River, built to monitor the Comanche and Kiowa Nations and to protect travelers on the Santa Fe Trail. Site of a treaty between the U.S. government and local Indigenous nations. Historic marker is 4 miles west of Dodge City.
Fort Aubrey	1865–66	Short-lived post constructed after the Civil War to protect pioneers and stagecoach lines from Indigenous raids near present-day Syracuse. Constructed on a former military site used after as a resting station for western troops.
Fort Belmont	1860–64	Fort built near present-day Buffalo to protect settlers from Missouri border ruffians during the Bleeding Kansas unrest. Occupied during the Civil War by a local militia and Creek Indian refugees.
Fort Brooks	ca. 1864	Temporary fort built near present-day Clyde by the local militia in response to Indigenous unrest. Protected settlements from raids and acted as a local headquarters for defense against Indians.

Fort Clifton	1862–63	Small fort erected by local settlers during the Civil War as a defense against Indians. Exact site lost; thought to have been near Fort Brooks.
Fort Dodge	1865–82	Military fort built east of present-day Dodge City, to protect wagon trains along the Santa Fe Trail and as a base of operations during the Indian Wars.
Fort Downer	1865–68	Originally a stage station near present-day Wakeeney. Converted into a military post after an 1865 Indian massacre. Protected the stage route and used by Gen. George Custer during his operations against the Indians in 1867.
Fort Harker (Fort Ellsworth)	1864–72	Military post established to protect frontier settlements. Later used to supply and protect railroad construction crews. Buildings remain, one housing a museum, in Kanopolis.
Fort Hays	1865–89	Military post that protected roads, defended railroad workers, guarded U.S. mail and travelers, and supplied army posts in western Kansas. Buildings are preserved at Fort Hays State Historic Site in Hays.
Fort Jewell	1870	Hastily built and then abandoned by local settlers in response to false rumors that the Cheyennes were preparing for war. Historic marker is in Jewell.

Fort Larned	1859–78	Key military post during the Indian Wars. Protected the Santa Fe Trail and later served as a distribution center for annuities promised to Indians. Fort Larned National Historic Site is 6 miles west of Larned.
Fort Mann	1847–48	Station on the Santa Fe Trail halfway between Fort Leavenworth and Santa Fe, occupied by military teamsters to repair wagons. Historic marker is west of Dodge City.
Fort Montgomery	1861–68	Constructed in Eureka by local settlers as protection against Indians, proslavery forces, and Confederate guerrillas during the Civil War.
Fort Monument	1865–68	Originally established as a station on the stage and mail route. Converted to a military station that protected transportation routes in response to violent encounters with Indians. What little remains is near the Gove County boundary, about 1 mile southwest of Monument Rocks.
Fort Riley	1852–present	Military base built between present-day Junction City and Manhattan to protect pioneers and traders along the Oregon, California, and Santa Fe Trails. Stationed troops during Bleeding Kansas and the Indian Wars, served as a military base during the major wars of the twentieth century, and remains an important U.S. Army training and housing facility.

Fort Saunders	1855–56	Proslavery stronghold built southwest of present-day Lawrence during the Kansas-Missouri Border War. Served as a defensible headquarters for proslavery forces.
Fort Wallace	1865–82	Military fort that served as a rest station for travelers, monitored local Indians, and protected the stage route. Saw much action during the Indian Wars and was nicknamed the "Fightin'est Fort in the West." Fort Wallace Museum is in Wallace.
Fort Zarah	1864–69	Military fort established to guard the Santa Fe Trail and provide escorts for travelers because of frequent Indian attacks in the area. Historic marker is in Fort Zarah Park, Great Bend.

The Yellowstone and Missouri Rivers flow from the Rocky Mountains across the plains of eastern Montana. The geography made that region prime habitat for beavers, a feature noticed by Lewis and Clark and other early explorers of the area. Additionally, the Montana plains are ideal habitat for bison, a resource vital to the powerful Native nations that flourished there. Further, Montana's mountains have rich gold deposits. The forts of Montana are, with few exceptions, related to these three resources and the people who exploited them. In the early and mid-1800s fur companies built forts to facilitate trade with Indigenous, American, Canadian, and European beaver trappers. Following the Civil War, forts were erected to monitor the Northern Cheyennes, Assiniboines, Blackfeet, Absarokas (Crows), Lakota Sioux, and other nations. From these forts, the military forced Indian removal to reservations. Soldiers stationed at forts also protected the trails that led into Montana's goldfields. The Missouri River could be navigated by steamboat to Fort Benton, the farthest inland port in the United States.

Fort	Years of operation	Description
Fort Alexander	1842–50	Trading post established near Forsyth by the American Fur Company. Abandoned in favor of Fort Sarpy in 1850. No trace remains.
Fort Assiniboine	1879–1911	Military fort built near the Canadian border after American defeats in the Great Sioux War. Constructed to prevent Sioux and Nez Perce attacks from the north and Chief Sitting Bull's return to the United States from Canada. One original building remains at Fort Assiniboine State Historic Site near Havre.
Fort Belknap	1867–88	Established as a trading post in present-day Harlem. Later used as a station on the Great Northern Railroad and converted into Fort Belknap Indian Reservation headquarters in 1888.
Fort Benton (Fort Lewis)	ca. 1847–81	American Fur Company base of operations at the westernmost navigable point on the Missouri River. Later leased by the U.S. government as a military post and housed peace talks between local Indian nations and settlers. Old Fort Benton is in Fort Benton.

Fort Browning	1868–73	Government trading post near present-day Dodson. Became the Indian agency for the Assiniboines and Upper Sioux. Site of a smallpox outbreak in 1869.
Fort Campbell	ca. 1847–60	Missouri Fur Company trading post built at a strategic location 1 mile from Fort Benton to compete with the American Fur Company. Historic marker is in present-day Fort Benton Historic District.
Fort Carroll	1874–82	Trading post and steamboat landing built by the Diamond R Transportation Company south of Zortman to move freight and passengers from the Missouri River to Helena.
Fort Cass	1832–35	American Fur Company trading post built on the Yellowstone River north of Bighorn to facilitate trade with the Crow Nation.
Fort C. F. Smith	1866–68	One of several military forts constructed along the Bozeman Trail to protect wagons heading to goldfields in Montana during Red Cloud's War. Make arrangements to visit fort ruins on private land at Yellowtail Dam Visitor Center near present-day Fort Smith.

Fort Chardon	1844–45	Short-lived American Fur Company trading post built on the Missouri River. Abandoned when nearby Fort Lewis was built. Historic marker is near Big Sandy.
Fort Claggett (Camp Cook)	1866–70	Military fort built to monitor the Blackfeet Indians, protect Missouri River traffic, and defend emigrants moving into Montana's goldfields. Fort's stone building remains at American Prairie Reserve near Winifred.
Fort Conrad	1875–78	American Fur Company stockaded trading post built on the Marias River. Fort Conrad Historical Monument Park is near Naismith.
Fort Copelin	ca. 1865–1867	Built as a privately operated trading post and supply depot on the Milk River near present-day Nashua for the steamboat travel of the Montana and Idaho Transportation Line.
Fort Cotton	1842	Short-lived trading post established in present-day Chouteau County by Fox, Livingston & Company on the site that later became Fort Lewis.
Fort Custer	1877–98	Military fort established by the U.S. Army to monitor the Crow Indians. Housed troops used in various campaigns of the Indian Wars. Historic marker in Hardin.

Fort Dauphin	1860–65	Privately owned trading post near the mouth of the Milk River south of present-day Nashua. Closed after its founder, Louis Dauphin, was killed by Sioux in 1865.
Fort Ellis	1867–86	Military post built east of Bozeman to protect settlers and miners from Indians and house soldiers during the Indian Wars. Base for early visitors to Yellowstone. Historic marker is in Bozeman.
Fort Fox-Livingston	1842–44	Trading post established by Fox, Livingston & Company near Fort Benton to compete with the American Fur Company. Later bought by their rivals.
Fort Galpin	ca. 1862–64	Trading post established by LaBarge, Harkness & Company on the Missouri River near present-day Fort Peck.
Fort Gilbert	1864–67	Trading post built in eastern Montana at southern edge of Fort Buford Military Reservation. Supplied settlers in the Yellowstone River valley. Historic marker is north of Sidney.
Fort Hawley	1866	Trading post established by the North West Company on the Missouri River near Fort Benton to support trade with the Crow Indians.

Fort Henry	1822–23	Fur-trading post at the junction on the Missouri and Yellowstone Rivers southwest of present-day Williston, North Dakota, destroyed by Indians soon after its construction.
Fort Howes	1897	Small, temporary rock-walled fortification built as a refuge for settlers in 1897. Structure remains on BLM Fort Howes Fire Station near Ashland.
Fort Jackson	1833–34	American Fur Company trading post built on the Missouri River near the mouth of the Poplar River in present-day Roosevelt County, abandoned the following year.
Fort Janeaux	1879–83	Trading post built by Francis Janeaux and his wife. Exchanged bison robes, furs, and meat. Grew into the town of Lewistown.
Fort Keogh	1876–1924	Military post built shortly after the Battle of the Little Bighorn in present-day Miles City to launch military campaigns against Indians. Later served as an army remount station and as a quartermaster's depot during World War I. The Range Riders Museum is housed in one of four remaining buildings in Miles City.

Fort LaBarge	1862–63	Trading post established by LaBarge, Harkness & Company on the Missouri River to compete with the American Fur Company. Dry conditions and low river levels caused its bankruptcy in 1863. Historic marker is in Fort Benton.
Fort Lewis	1845–60	American Fur Company trading post on the Missouri River, built to facilitate trade with Blackfeet Indians. Name changed to Fort Benton when moved to a preferred location downstream.
Fort Logan	1869–80	Military fort built to protect nearby mining camps and the Fort Benton freight road from Indians. Housed troops for many campaigns of the Indian Wars in western Montana. Remains including the blockhouse are northwest of White Sulphur Springs.
Fort Maginnis	1880–90	Established to protect cattlemen from raiding Blackfeet and Sioux. Last of a line of five forts built after the defeat of Gen. George Custer at the Battle of the Little Bighorn. Ruins remain northeast of Lewistown.
Fort McKenzie	1832–44	Built by the American Fur Company on the Missouri River near present-day Loma to trade with the Blackfeet. Eventually replaced by Fort Chardon.

Fort Mortimer	1842–46	Union Fur Company trading post built east of the remains of Fort William at the mouth of the Yellowstone River to compete with the American Fur Company. Sold to the rival business in 1846.
Fort Parker	1869–75	Built by the U.S. government as a refuge for the Crows from the Sioux. Also known as the First Crow Agency, the site has been preserved near the Yellowstone River east of present-day Livingston.
Fort Pease	1875–76	Established as a trading post and expected riverboat landing but held under siege by the Sioux. U.S. Army intervened and briefly occupied the fort during the Sioux Wars. Historic marker is in Hysham.
Fort Peck	1867–77	Trading post of the Durfee & Peck Trading Company. Became the Milk River Indian Agency for the Assiniboine and Sioux tribes near present-day Fort Peck.
Fort Piegan	1831–32	Wintering station built by the American Fur Company. Facilitated trade with the Blackfeet until spring, when they burned it down. Historic marker is near Loma.

Fort Sarpy	1850–60	Trading post built on the Yellowstone River east of Forsyth by the American Fur Company to replace Fort Alexander and facilitate trade with the Crows.
Fort Shaw	1867–91	Military fort built to protect the freight road from Fort Benton to Helena and growing mining settlements. Also served as a base for Indian Wars campaigns. Portions of the fort survive as a military cemetery and small museum near present-day Fort Shaw.
Fort Van Buren	1835–42	Trading post built by the American Fur Company on the Yellowstone River near present-day Rosebud. Replaced by Fort Alexander in 1842.
Fort William Henry Harrison	1892–present	Several smaller posts were combined into this military fort near Helena in 1892. In 1922 it became a training site for the Montana National Guard, a role it currently holds.

In the 1830s Nebraska became a gateway to the West as the Oregon Trail, and later the California and Mormon Trails followed the Platte River across the state. Earlier, trappers had explored, searching for beavers, and built trading posts to promote trade. Even earlier, the Pawnees and other powerful tribes hunted the innumerable bison that migrated seasonally across the plains. Forts were constructed to protect trappers, traders, emigrants crossing Nebraska, and finally settlers homesteading in the state. From these forts, soldiers waged war against Native nations in the years after the Civil War.

Fort	Years of operation	Description
Fort Atkinson	1819–27	Built on a site recommended by William Clark, the first U.S. fort west of the Missouri River on the eastern fringe of the Great Plains. Protected the fledgling American fur trade and promoted peaceful relations between traders and Indians. Fort Atkinson State Historical Park is in Fort Calhoun.
Fort Grattan	1855	Military post intended to provide protection for emigrants and mail delivery during the Sioux Wars but abandoned after only three weeks.
Fort Hartsuff	1874–81	Military fort established after Sioux Indians attacked settlers in the region. Protected settlers and provided refuge for the Pawnees in their conflict with the Sioux. Fort Hartsuff State Historical Park is in Burwell.
Fort Kearny	1848–71	Important military fort on the Oregon Trail that protected emigrants and Indians; housed a post office, Pony Express station, stagecoach station, and telegraph station; and provided fresh livestock. Fort Kearny State Historical Park is in Kearny.

Fort Lisa	1812–23	Influential trading post established by Manuel Lisa on the Missouri River for the Missouri Fur Company. Became an important trading hub. Historic marker is in northern Omaha.
Fort McPherson	1863–80	Military fort that protected the overland emigrant trains, stagecoaches, mail delivery, and telegraph lines. Several campaigns launched from this fort during the Indian Wars. Fort and historic marker are in North Platte.
Fort Mitchell	1864–67	Small sod military outpost built on the North Platte River in western Nebraska. Manned by volunteer cavalry who protected overland travelers during the Civil War. Two historic markers are in Mitchell.
Plum Creek Station	1864–67	Pony Express station southeast of present-day Lexington, converted into a military garrison that protected emigrants and stagecoaches between Fort Kearny and Fort McPherson.
Fort Robidoux	ca. 1822–40	Trading post established by the American Fur Company on the Missouri River in present-day northern Omaha. Provisioned nearby Fort Atkinson and resupplied explorers and trappers moving upstream.

| Fort Robinson | 1874–1948 | Military fort important during the Sioux Wars. The site where thousands of Lakotas under Crazy Horse surrendered and where he died. Cheyenne and Sioux Reservation monitored from this site. Quartermaster depot during World War I and remained active through World War II. Fort Robinson History Center is in Crawford. |
| Fort Sidney | 1867–94 | Military fort established to protect the Union Pacific Railroad and serve as a supply depot for prospectors and miners moving into the Black Hills. Fort Sidney Museum is in Sidney. |

The southwest fringe of the Great Plains stretches into eastern New Mexico before butting up against the Rocky Mountains. Here a handful of forts were constructed to assist travelers on the Santa Fe Trail, suppress Native nations, and protect a growing number of settlers on the southwestern plains.

Fort	Years of operation	Description
Fort Bascom	1863–70	Built to suppress the Comanches and Kiowas and stop the trade in stolen goods near the Texas border. Historic marker is 10 miles north of Tucumcari.
Fort Burgwin	1852–60	Fort on the western fringe of the plains established to monitor Ute and Jicarilla Apaches in the Taos Valley. Reconstructed fort and historic marker are in Ranchos de Taos.
Fort Stanton	1855–1953	Military fort on the fringe of the plains built to defend settlers on the Rio Bonito during the Apache wars. Seized by Confederates during the Civil War. Repurposed in 1899, serving as a military hospital and housing German and Japanese Americans considered "troublemakers" during World War II. Fort Stanton Historic Site is outside Lincoln. Museum and visitor center are in Fort Stanton.
Fort Sumner	1863–68	Built to protect settlers on the Pecos River and monitor Mescalero Apaches, Kiowas, Comanches, and Navajos on the nearby Redondo Reservation. Fort Sumner Historic Site and marker and Bosque Redondo Memorial are in Fort Sumner.
Fort Union	1851–91	Established on the Santa Fe Trail on the western fringe of the Great Plains to outfit travelers on the trail. Later the home of the Ninth Cavalry during the Apache wars. Fort Union National Monument is in Watrous.

NORTH DAKOTA

Like many other Great Plains states, North Dakota has a long history of Indigenous peoples, trappers, emigrants, and homesteaders who survived and thrived in a difficult environment. Forts played a key role in this process, from Fort Mandan, constructed by Lewis and Clark during the winter of 1804–5, to Fort Yates, built to monitor the Sioux Nation and remaining in use into the twentieth century. The forts facilitated trade with Natives and served as the launch pads for military campaigns during the Indian Wars.

Fort	Years of operation	Description
Fort Abercrombie	ca. 1858–77	First permanent U.S. military fort in North Dakota. Protected settlers in the Red River valley from the Sioux Indians and supplied trappers and travelers heading north and west. Fort Abercrombie State Historic Site is in Abercrombie.
Fort Abraham Lincoln	1872–91	Military fort initially established on the Missouri River to protect survey crews and railway workers. Troops stationed there participated in several campaigns against Indians, including the Battle of the Little Bighorn. Fort Abraham Lincoln State Park's reconstructed buildings are near Mandan.
Fort Berthold I	1845–62	American Fur Company trading post built on the Missouri River and burned by the Sioux in 1862. Original site is under the waters of Lake Sakakawea, created by the Garrison Dam.
Fort Berthold II (Fort Atkinson)	ca. 1858–70	Trading post built by an independent trapper and purchased by the American Fur Company when Fort Berthold I was burned. Housed a small garrison of soldiers from 1864 to 1870, when the region became an Indian reservation. Original site is under the waters of Lake Sakakawea.

Fort Buford	1866–95	Military fort built at the confluence of the Missouri and Yellowstone Rivers to protect emigrants. Grew in importance as conflict with Indians increased in the 1870s, becoming a key supply point for troops during the Black Hills War. Fort Buford State Historic Site is near Williston.
Fort Clark	1830–61	Trading post of the American Fur Company built along the Missouri River just south of a Mandan Indian village. Became a source of smallpox and cholera outbreaks that decimated Mandan and Arikara populations. Fort Clark State Historic Site is near Fort Clark.
Fort Dilts	1864	Sod fort built during a 16-day siege by Lakota Indians of a wagon train of miners in September 1864, which ended when reinforcements arrived to help the miners. Fort Dilts State Historic Site is northwest of Rhame.
Fort Mandan	1804–5	Built by the Lewis and Clark Expedition as a winter headquarters near a Mandan Indian village and used for five months as the expedition prepared to continue its journey, enlisting the help of Sacagawea. Fort Mandan State Historic Site is in Washburn.
Fort Pembina	1870–95	Military fort built where a series of trading posts had existed since the 1780s in response to unrest in the Red River valley. It protected settlers from the Sioux and patrolled for smugglers between the United States and Canada. Pembina State Museum is in Pembina.

Fort Ransom	1867–72	Military fort constructed to protect settlers and railroad workers from the Sioux and to patrol the emigrant trail from Minnesota to Montana. Fort Ransom State Historic Site and historic marker are southwest of Fort Ransom.
Fort Rice	1864–78	First of a chain of forts that protected land and river routes from the Sioux. Used for Indian negotiations and garrisoned by converted Confederate soldiers who had been taken prisoner. Fort Rice State Historic Site and historic marker are south of Mandan.
Fort Seward	1872–77	Military fort built to protect settlers and Northern Pacific Railroad construction workers, patrol telegraph lines, and enforce the law. Fort Seward Historic Site is in Jamestown.
Fort Stevenson	1867–83	Military fort that stored supplies for other military posts in the Dakota Territory and protected vessels traveling on the Missouri River. Fort Stevenson State Park is south of Garrison.
Fort Totten	1867–90	Built to protect the Totten Trail, an overland route extending across the Dakota Territory, later protecting the Totten Indian Reservation and serving as a boarding school. Fort Totten State Historic Site is in Fort Totten.

Fort Union	1828–67	Important American Fur Company trading post at the confluence of the Yellowstone and Missouri Rivers. Controlled the bison robe and fur trade until occupied by the military in 1864. Dismantled in 1867, the materials used to build Fort Buford. The rebuilt Fort Union Trading Post National Historic Site is near Williston.
Fort William	1833–36, 1858–66	Trading post established at the confluence of the Missouri and Yellowstone Rivers near Buford by fur trappers William Sublette and Robert Campbell, who soon sold it to the American Fur Company. Closed in 1836 and rebuilt in a new location in 1858. Historic marker is in Williston.
Fort Yates	1863–1903	Military fort that oversaw several bands of the Sioux tribe. Fort's land ceded to the Sioux in 1868 but military remained until 1903. Fort Yates is the Sioux tribe's headquarters on the Standing Rock Reservation.

Known as Indian Territory for much of the nineteenth century, Oklahoma is the ancestral home of numerous Indian nations, and many emigrant Native Nations were forced to move there from their traditional homelands east of the Mississippi. Forts were hubs of diplomatic activity where relocated Indians traded, received allotments, and sought protection from rivals. Indian Territory was a battleground during the Civil War, with both the Confederacy and the Union building and occupying fortifications. After the Civil War, forts were used to launch military campaigns against the Indians of the southern plains.

Fort	Years of operation	Description
Fort Arbuckle	1851–70	Military fort that protected travelers along emigrant trails and defended the relocated Chickasaw from displaced Comanche Indians. Historic site and marker are near Davis.
Fort Cobb	1859–69	Military fort established to supervise the relocation of Texas Indians into Oklahoma. Occupied by both Confederate and Union forces during the Civil War and later served as a post for soldiers during the Indian Wars. Historic marker is in Fort Cobb.
Fort Coffee	1834–38	Military fort built to stop whiskey shipments up the Arkansas River into Indian Territory and protect newly relocated Indians. Historic marker is east of Spiro.
Fort Davis	1861–62	Confederate headquarters in Indian Territory during the Civil War, built to hold Indian Territory and prevent Union invasions. Abandoned after the Confederate defeat at the Battle of Pea Ridge. Historic marker is in Muskogee.
Fort Gibson	1824–90	Union headquarters in Indian Territory during the Civil War, originally built to keep peace between the Osages and Cherokees. Starting point for several military expeditions that explored the West. Fort Gibson Historic Site is in Fort Gibson.

Fort McCulloch	1862–65	Confederate military fort built on the Blue River after Confederate troops withdrew from Fort Davis, serving as a refuge for Confederate sympathizers. Cherokee Confederate general Stand Watie's command post in 1865. Historic marker is west of Kenefic.
Fort Reno	1874–1949	Military fort that managed the Southern Cheyenne and Southern Arapaho Reservations. Closed in 1908 but soon reactivated. Used as a remount station and remained in operation until after World War II. Fort Reno Visitors Center is in El Reno, and a historic marker is west of town.
Fort Sill	1869–present	Military fort built during the Indian Wars to discourage Indian raids into Texas and Kansas. Later housed field artillery regiments and eventually became the permanent home of the U.S. Army Field Artillery School. Fort Sill National Historic Landmark and Museum are north of Lawton.
Fort Supply	1868–94	Built to support a campaign against the Cheyennes. Later defended the Cheyenne and Arapaho Reservations from incursions by white settlers. Fort Supply Historic Site is in Fort Supply.

Fort Towson	1824–29, 1831–54	Military fort built to guard the U.S. border with Spanish-controlled Texas, oversee the relocation of the Choctaws into Indian Territory, and maintain law and order in the region. Surrendered by Confederate general Stand Watie to Union troops in June 1865. Fort Towson Historic Site is northeast of Fort Towson.
Fort Washita	1842–65	Constructed to protect the Choctaws and Chickasaws from rival nations. Guarded the Texas frontier, staged troops during the Mexican-American War, and was occupied by Confederate troops during the Civil War. Fort Washita Historic Site and Museum are in Durant.
Fort Wayne	1838–42, 1861–62	Built to protect roads and diminish the fear of Cherokee in the area. Rebuilt during the Civil War and occupied by the Confederate Cherokee Mounted Rifles until captured by Union troops early in the war. Historic marker is near Jay.

South Dakota was named for the Lakota, Nakota, and Dakota Sioux, powerful Indigenous confederacies that spread west from the Great Lakes after acquiring horses. These peoples came into conflict with the Mandans, Hidatsas, Arikaras, and other nations living along the Missouri River and its tributaries. The Missouri crosses through the center of the state and was a highway of the fur trade, which necessitated the construction of trading posts in South Dakota in the early 1800s, some of which were known as forts. Many of South Dakota's forts were built as settlers, miners, and railroads encroached on Indigenous lands. The U.S. government constructed most of the forts between 1860 and 1880 to wage war against the Sioux, who fought to protect their sacred Black Hills and other lands from the American invaders.

Fort	Years of operation	Description
Fort Bennett	ca. 1870–91	Military fort relocated four times during the Indian Wars to monitor the Sioux residents of the Cheyenne River Indian Agency. Site lies under the waters of Oahe Reservoir.
Fort Brulé	1862–68	Built by civilians during the Civil War as a refuge during the Dakota Uprising of 1862 and occupied briefly by soldiers before its closure. Historic site marker is near Richland.
Fort Dakota	1865–69	Military fort in a chain of posts from Minnesota to the Missouri River. Protected settlers and watched the Sioux country border. Historic marker is in Sioux Falls.
Fort Defiance	1845–51	Trading post built at the mouth of the Medicine Creek by former employees of the American Fur Company. Site is near Lower Brule, most likely under the waters of Lake Sharpe.
Fort Dole	1862	Built by the Yankton Indian Agency in present-day Greenwood during the Civil War to intercede between rival Sioux bands.
Fort Hale	ca. 1870–84	U.S. Army fort established on the Missouri River north of Chamberlain to observe the Lower Brulé Indian Agency and to protect settlers from the Sioux.

Fort James	1865–66	One of the few stone military forts built along the chain of posts guarding the frontier between settlers and Sioux Indian lands near present-day Rockport.
Fort Kiowa	1822–40s	Trading post on the Missouri River built by the Columbia Fur Company and fortified as a defense against Crow and Sioux attacks. Changed hands several times throughout its colorful history. Site is north of Chamberlain, now under the waters of Fort Randall Lake.
Lac Traverse Post	1817–23	Operated by the British Hudson's Bay Company near present-day White Rock to facilitate trade with Natives.
Fort Lookout	1831–63	Name given to two different forts that occupied the same site or nearby sites above Chamberlain: a Columbia Fur Company post and later an army post. Historic marker is at entrance to Lower Brule Indian Reservation near Reliance.
Fort Manuel	1812–13	Established by fur trade pioneer Manuel Lisa on the Big Bend of the Missouri River. Destroyed by British allied tribal nations during the War of 1812. Sacagawea said to have died here. Original site on Standing Rock Indian Reservation lies under the Missouri's Oahe Reservoir waters. Reconstructed fort and historic marker are nearby in Kenel.

Fort Meade	ca. 1878–1944	Military fort established to protect the Black Hills mining district and monitor the Sioux Indians. Operated as a military post until 1944. Old Fort Meade Museum and historic marker are in Fort Meade.
Fort Pierre	1832–57	Independently operated fur-trading post purchased by the military in 1855 and serving as an army post for two years. Site with stone marker is a national historic landmark just north of present-day Fort Pierre.
Fort Randall	1856–92	Military fort that replaced Fort Pierre and was an important base during the Indian Wars. Guarded the Platte River overland trails and Missouri River traffic. Located near Pickstown.
Fort Recovery	1822–30	Missouri Fur Company trading post built on American Island on the Missouri River near Chamberlain at the site of two previous trading posts. Fort site is now under the waters of Fort Randall Lake.
Fort Sisseton (Fort Wadsworth)	1864–89	Military fort built to suppress fighting among local Indian tribes, protect settlements, and guard the northern wagon route to the goldfields of Idaho and Montana. Fort Sisseton Historic State Park and historic marker are in Lake City.
Fort Sod	1858	Temporary sod-walled enclosure where settlers took refuge during a period of Indian uprisings. Site of a six-week Sioux siege. Site and historic markers in Sioux Falls.

Old Fort Sully, Fort Sully	1863–66, 1866–94	Important military fort on the Missouri River, serving as a base during campaigns of the Indian Wars. Relocated in 1866 and continued to be used to monitor relations between settlers and Indians. Farm Island Visitor Center is on Old Fort Sully footprint near Pierre; old fort's historic marker is east of Pierre. New Fort Sully site was inundated by Lake Oahe; historic marker is in Onida.
Fort Thompson	1864–67	Military fort that served as agency headquarters for the Creek Indian Reservation. Historic marker is near present-day Fort Thompson.
Fort Vermillion	1833–51	Trading post built on the Missouri River near the mouth of the Vermillion River by the American Fur Company. Historic marker is in Burbank.
Fort Whetstone	1870–72	Military fort located on the Whetstone Indian Reservation to protect the agency and monitor the Sioux Indians. Site near Bonesteel is now underwater.
Fort Yankton	1862	Built by civilian residents of Sioux Falls during the Civil War in response to the Sioux Uprising of 1862. Historic site marker is in present-day Yankton.

In addition to the powerful Indian nations that have called Texas home for centuries, five national flags have flown over the state: those of Spain, Mexico, Texas, the United States, and the Confederate States. Each of these nations created presidios or forts for various purposes. Some forts were built to guard a single settlement. Under the Texas and later the U.S. flags, chains of forts marked, monitored, and protected the Texas frontier from the Rio Grande in the south to the Red River in the north. Forts marked a border between the Kiowas, Comanches, Apaches, and other Native nations to the west and Texan and American settlers to the east. As the frontier moved westward, some forts closed and new forts opened. During the Civil War, federal troops pulled out of Texas forts, and many of them were occupied by Confederate forces until the demands of the war drew them away as well. Many were reoccupied after the Civil War, and some were linked by telegraph lines by the mid-1870s. A few Texas forts have remained in use into the twentieth and twenty-first centuries.

Fort Name	Years of operation	Description
The Alamo	1718–1836	Built in present-day San Antonio to house Spanish missionaries and soldiers. Site of the famous Battle of the Alamo in 1836 during Texas's war for independence from Mexico. Free timed entry for visitors.
Fort Belknap	1851–67	The northern anchor of frontier defenses against Kiowa and Comanche raiders. Protected travelers and settlers and became a transportation hub in northern Texas. Historic site is in Newcastle.
Bird's Fort	1841–42	Built by the Texas militia in present-day El Paso to guard the frontier and encourage settlement. Site of a major treaty between Texas and many Indian nations.
Fort Bliss	1854–present	Established to monitor Apaches but repurposed throughout its long history. Current home of the First Armored Division, used for missile and artillery training and as a military operational intelligence center.
Fort Chadbourne	1852–67	U.S. military fort on the line of frontier defenses. Guarded the Butterfield Overland Mail route. Taken by Confederates in 1861 and retaken by Union troops in 1865. Historic military post and marker are in Bronte.

Fort Clark	1852–1946	Prominent military fort that monitored the Mexican border and guarded the El Paso Road. Buffalo Soldiers and Black Seminole Indian Scouts billeted there. During World War II the last horse cavalry trained and German prisoners of war incarcerated at fort. Fort Clark Historic District is in Brackettville.
Fort Coleman (Fort Colorado)	1836–38	Built on the frontier by Texas Rangers during Texas's independence to defend against Kiowa and Comanche raiders and launch campaigns against the Indians. Historic marker is in Austin.
Fort Concho	1867–89	Adobe military fort that replaced Fort Chadbourne after the Civil War. Part of the frontier defense system, guarded mail, wagon, and stagecoach lines and the local settlement of San Angelo. Fort Concho National Historic Landmark District is in San Angelo.
Camp Cooper	1856–61	Built by Texas near present-day Albany to protect the frontier and monitor the nearby Comanche Reservation. Headquarters of cavalry under Robert E. Lee and abandoned at start of Civil War. Historic marker is west of Throckmorton.
Fort Croghan	1849–55	Center of a line of U.S. military forts built on the Texas frontier. Housed Texas Rangers to protect nearby settlements from Comanche and Apache raiders. Fort Croghan Museum is in Burnet.

Fort Davis	1854–91	Built on the western fringe of the Great Plains by the U.S. War Department to guard the southern mail and wagon route. Fort Davis National Historic Site is in Fort Davis.
Fort Duncan	ca. 1849–1945	Military fort built on the Rio Grande to monitor trade on the Mexican border. Used periodically, most recently as an officers' club and swimming pool during World War II. Fort Duncan Museum is in Eagle Pass.
Fort Elliott	1875–90	Military fort built to drive Indians from the Texas Panhandle and promote settlement. Fort's presence accelerated cattle ranching. Fort and Buffalo Soldiers at Fort Elliott historic markers are near Mobeetie.
Fort Gates	1849–52	Military fort in the line of defense. Protected settlers on the frontier from Indians and encouraged further settlement. Historic marker is at fort site near Gatesville.
Fort Goliad (Presidio La Bahia)	1749–1836	Constructed by Spain to protect missions in southern Texas from Indian raids and French invasion. Site of the Goliad Massacre during Texas's war for independence. Presidio–La Bahia historic site is in Goliad.
Fort Graham	1849–53	Military fort established in the northwestern part of the frontier defense system. Protected settlers from Kiowa and Comanche raiders. Historic marker is near Whitney.

Fort Griffin (Camp Wilson)	1867–81	Established after the Civil War for added frontier protection from Kiowa and Comanche raiders. Replaced Fort Belknap and became the starting point for emigrants traveling westward on the southern route. Fort Griffin State Historic Site is near Albany.
Fort Hood	1942–present	Military base established during World War II near Killeen to test and train tank destroyers and hold prisoners of war. Remains one of the largest and most populous military installations in the world.
Fort Inge	1849–69	Military fort established in the southwestern part of the frontier defense system to protect settlers and the overland mail route from Comanche and Apache raiders. Fort Inge Historical Park is near Uvalde.
Fort Inglish	1837–43	Private fort constructed by settler Bailey Inglish. Used by the Army of the Republic of Texas during campaigns against the Indians. Fort Inglish Village is in Bonham.
Fort Johnson	1840–41	Built by the Republic of Texas as the northernmost military fort in the line of frontier posts to defend the military road from Austin to Red River. Abandoned soon after its construction. Historic site marker is in Pottsborough.

Fort Lancaster	1855–61 ca. 1871–73	U.S. military fort protecting the road from San Antonio to El Paso and emigrants journeying to California. Abandoned in 1861 but reoccupied briefly 10 years later. Fort Lancaster State Historic Site is in Sheffield.
Fort Lincoln	1849–52	Military fort built as part of the frontier line defenses. Protected settlers and goods transported on the Woll Road. Historic site marker is near D'Hanis.
Little River Fort	1836–41	Built during Texas's independence to guard the Little River settlement. Site of two skirmishes with the Comanches. Historic marker is near Belton.
Fort Martin Scott	1848–66	Military fort constructed as part of the first line of federal frontier defenses. Protected the road between Fredericksburg and San Antonio. Fort Martin Scott Historic Site is in Fredericksburg.
Fort Mason	1848–69	Military fort established as Texas's population grew after U.S. annexation. Played an important role in westward settlement. Fort Mason is in Mason.
Fort McIntosh	1851–1946	Military fort built on the Rio Grande to police the Mexican border. Served many purposes, including monitoring Indians, housing Buffalo Soldiers, training World War I recruits, and housing soldiers during World War II. Fort McIntosh Historic District is in Laredo.

Fort McKavett	1852–83	Military fort, originally called Camp San Saba, built to protect frontier travelers and settlers from the Indians. Served as a supply base for western Texas and a testing site for new weapons and equipment. Fort McKavett State Historic Site is in Fort McKavett.
Fort Merrill	1850–55	Military fort situated on a ford of the Nueces River as part of the defensive frontier line, but garrisoned only intermittently until its closure. Historic site marker is near Dinero.
Fort Milam (Fort Viesca)	ca. 1834–39	Military fort built on the Brazos River by Texans during their war for independence to protect Saraville de Viesca from Comanche raiders. Historic site marker is near Marlin.
Fort Parker	1834–36	Privately constructed by the Parker family. Site of an 1836 Comanche and Kiowa raid that left many family members dead or kidnapped. Old Fort Parker Historic Site is near Groesbeck.
Fort Phantom Hill	1851–54	Military fort that was part of the second federal line of frontier forts. Protected travelers during its short life and later repurposed as a mail and stagecoach way station and a Confederate battalion. Historic Fort Phantom Hill is in Abilene.

Fort Richardson	1867–78	Northernmost military fort in the line of federal forts established after the Civil War. Protected settlers against Comanche and Kiowa raiders as the settlements expanded north and west. Fort Richardson State Park and Historic Site are in Jacksboro.
Fort Ringgold	1848–1944	Military fort built on the Mexican border at the end of the Mexican-American War to bring law and order to the region and as the southernmost in the line of defense. Operated sporadically until World War II. Historic marker is at Fort Ringgold main entrance in Rio Grande City.
Fort Sam Houston	ca. 1845–present	Military fort built near San Antonio to establish a U.S. military presence in Texas before its annexation. Used to mobilize the Rough Riders during the Spanish-American War. Home of the first Women's Army Auxiliary Corps. Joined with Lackland and Randolph Air Force Base to create Joint Base San Antonio under Air Force administration in San Antonio. Remains a major U.S. military base today.
Presidio de San Saba	1757–72	Built by Spanish officials to protect Mission Santa Cruz de San Saba and strengthen Spain's claim to the region. Mission was destroyed by Comanche and Wichita raiders before the presidio's completion. Presidio de San Saba is near Menard.

Fort St. Louis	1685–89	Colony established by French settlers near the Gulf Coast. Plagued by disease, raids, and isolation, it failed within a few years. Later site of a Spanish presidio. Historic marker is in Inez.
Fort Stockton	1859–86	Military fort built at Comanche Springs as part of the defensive frontier system to protect stagecoach, freight, and mail routes. Home of Buffalo Soldiers after the Civil War. Historic Fort Stockton is in Fort Stockton.
Fort Terrett	1852–54	Military fort established on the North Llano River to defend settlements and travelers along the San Antonio Road from Comanche raids. Historic site marker is between Sonora and Junction.
Fort Worth	1849–53	Military fort built shortly after the Mexican-American War on the Trinity River as part of the line of frontier forts. Grew into the present-day city of Fort Worth. Historic marker is in Fort Worth.

The Great Plains cover the eastern half of Wyoming. Here the Cheyennes, Arapahos, Crows, and other Indian nations of the central plains encountered trappers searching for beaver-rich waters. Forts were constructed to facilitate trade in this remote region. Later, four to five hundred thousand emigrants crossed the plains of Wyoming, converging on South Pass before continuing on to Oregon, California, or Utah. Transcontinental railroad construction brought workers into the region. As the bison herds were decimated and the Native nations were forced onto reservations, most forts were abandoned.

Fort	Years of operation	Description
Fort Bernard	1845–66	Built to replace Fort Platte to facilitate trade with emigrants on the Oregon Trail before they reached nearby Fort Laramie. Commemorated by the Western History Center in nearby Lingle.
Fort Caspar	ca. 1862–67	Military fort built to defend a major North Platte River crossing on the Oregon, Mormon, and California Trails and protect mail service and newly constructed telegraph lines from Cheyenne and Lakota raiders. The Fort Caspar Museum is in city of Casper.
Fort Clay	1855–56	Military outpost built to protect Reshaw's Bridge, a North Platte River crossing on the Oregon, Mormon, and California Trails. Reshaw's Bridge has been reconstructed in Evansville.
Fort D. A. Russell	1867–present	Military base built to protect Union Pacific railroad workers. Became a permanent military post in 1884, serving as a cavalry base and later an airfield. Renamed Francis E. Warren Air Force Base in 1949 and was an important missile base during Cold War. Air base is adjacent to Cheyenne.

Fort Fetterman	1867–82	Established on the North Platte River as the northernmost post in eastern Wyoming. Replaced Fort Caspar as a supply point and staging area for army expeditions during the Indian Wars. The Fort Fetterman State Historic Site is near Douglas.
Fort Fred Steele	1868–86	Military fort built to protect railroad workers from Sioux and Cheyenne attacks and establish law and order in the region. Fort Fred Steele State Historic Site is off Interstate 80 near Sinclair.
Fort Laramie (Fort William)	1834–90	Fur-trading post built by William Sublette and later purchased by the U.S. Army. Became an important supply depot for emigrants on the Oregon, Mormon, and California Trails, with soldiers protecting travelers and telegraph lines and waging war on the Cheyenne and Lakota Nations. Fort Laramie National Historic Site is east of Guernsey.
Fort McKinney	1876–94	U.S. Army post established on the Powder River shortly after Gen. George Custer's defeat at Little Bighorn to monitor Sioux and Cheyenne activity and keep the peace among Crow, Arapaho, and Shoshone Nations. Fort McKinney, historic site marker, and Jim Gatchell Memorial Museum are in and near Buffalo.

Fort Phil Kearny	1866–68	Military fort that protected travelers on the Bozeman Trail, prevented intertribal warfare, and defended the Union Pacific Railroad lines. Fort Phil Kearny State Historic Site is near Banner.
Fort Platte	1840–46	Trading post built to compete with Fort Laramie. Closed when owners built nearby Fort Bernard. Historic site marker is near Fort Laramie.
Fort Reno (Fort Conner)	1865–68	Military fort that protected travelers on the Bozeman Trail, serving as a way station and supply depot for Fort Phil Kearny and Fort C. F. Smith. Historic site marker is between Kaycee and Sussex.
Fort Sanders	1866–82	Military fort built to protect the Overland Trail, an alternate route to other heavily traveled trails, and later used to defend railroad workers. Fort Sanders guardhouse and historic site marker are in Laramie.

SUGGESTED READING

Abel, Annie H., ed. *Chardon's Journal at Fort Clark, 1834–1839*. Lincoln: University of Nebraska Press, 1997.

Arkush, Elizabeth N., and Mark W. Allen, eds. *The Archaeology of Warfare: Prehistories of Raiding and Conquest*. Gainesville: University Press of Florida, 2006.

Athearn, Robert G. *Forts of the Upper Missouri*. Englewood Cliffs NJ: Prentice-Hall, 1967.

Ballard, Jack S. *Commander and Builder of Western Forts: The Life and Times of Major General Henry C. Merriam, 1862–1901*. College Station: Texas A&M University Press, 2012.

Barbour, Barton H. *Fort Union and the Upper Missouri Fur Trade*. Norman: University of Oklahoma Press, 2002.

Barnes, Jeff. *Forts of the Northern Plains: Guide to Historic Military Posts of the Plains Indian Wars*. Mechanicsburg PA: Stackpole, 2008.

Beckwourth, James P. *The Life and Adventures of James P. Beckwourth, as Told to Thomas D. Bonner*. Edited by Delmont Oswald. Lincoln: University of Nebraska Press, 1972.

Buckley, Jay H. *William Clark: Indian Diplomat*. Norman: University of Oklahoma Press, 2008.

Buckley, Jay H., and Jeffery D. Nokes. *Explorers of the American West: Mapping the World through Primary Documents*. Santa Barbara CA: ABC-CLIO, 2016.

Buckley, Jay H., and Brenden W. Rensink. *Historical Dictionary of the American Frontier*. Lanham MD: Rowman & Littlefield, 2015.

Burpee, Laurence J., ed. *Journals and Letters of Pierre Gaultier de Varennes de la Vérendrye and His Sons*. Vol. 16. Toronto: Champlain Society, 1927.

Clark, Andrew J., and Douglas B. Bamforth, eds. *Archaeological Perspectives on Warfare on the Great Plains*. Louisville: University Press of Colorado, 2018.

Frazer, Robert W. *Forts of the West: Military Forts and Presidios and Posts Commonly Called Forts West of the Mississippi River to 1898*. Norman: University of Oklahoma Press, 1965.

Hafen, LeRoy R. *Fort Laramie and the Pageant of the West, 1834–1890*. Lincoln: University of Nebraska Press, 1984.

———, ed. *The Mountain Men and the Fur Trade of the Far West*. 10 vols. Glendale CA: Arthur H. Clark, 1965–72.

Hannon, Leslie F. *Forts of Canada*. Toronto: McClelland and Stewart, 1969.

Hanson, James A. *When Skins Were Money: A History of the Fur Trade*. Chadron NE: Museum of the Fur Trade, 2005.

Harris, Matthew L., and Jay H. Buckley. *Zebulon Pike, Thomas Jefferson, and the Opening of the American West*. Norman: University of Oklahoma Press, 2012.

Harrison, Myron C. *Rescuing Beefsteak: The Story of a Pragmatic Pioneer Idealist*. Jackson Hole WY: self-published, 2018.

Hart, Herbert M. *Pioneer Forts of the West*. Seattle: Superior, 1967.

Hedren, Paul. *Traveler's Guide to the Great Sioux War: The Battlefields, Forts, and Related Sites of America's Greatest Indian War*. Helena: Montana Historical Society, 1996.

Innis, Harold A. *The Fur Trade of Canada*. Rev. ed. Toronto: University of Toronto Press, 1965.

Jones, David E. *Native North American Armor, Shields, and Fortifications*. Austin: University of Texas Press, 2004.

Lavender, David. *Bent's Fort*. Lincoln: University of Nebraska Press, 2013.

Lavin, Stephen J., Fred M. Shelley, and J. Clark Archer. *Atlas of the Great Plains*. Lincoln: University of Nebraska Press, 2011.

Magoffin, Susan Shelby. *Down the Santa Fe Trail and into Mexico: The Diary of Susan Shelby Magoffin, 1846–1847*. Edited by Stella M. Drumm. 1926. Reprint, Lincoln: University of Nebraska Press, 1982.

McDermott, John D. *A Guide to the Indian Wars of the West*. Lincoln: University of Nebraska Press, 1998.

Moorhead, Max L. *The Presidio: Bastion of the Spanish Borderlands*. Norman: University of Oklahoma Press, 1991.

Moulton, Gary E., ed. *The Journals of the Lewis & Clark Expedition*. Lincoln: University of Nebraska Press, 1983–2001.

Prucha, Francis Paul. *A Guide to the Military Posts of the United States, 1789–1895*. Madison: State Historical Society of Wisconsin, 1964.

Robertson, R. G. *Competitive Struggle: America's Western Fur Trading Posts, 1764–1865*. 2nd ed. Caldwell ID: Caxton, 2012.

Robinson, Ken. *Historic Tales of Whoop-Up Country: On the Trail from Montana's Fort Benton to Canada's Fort Macleod.* Charleston SC: History Press, 2020.

Robinson, Willard B. *American Forts: Architectural Form and Function.* Urbana: University of Illinois Press, 1977.

Schlesier, Karl H, ed. *Plains Indians, A.D. 500–1500: The Archaeological Past of Historic Groups.* Norman: University of Oklahoma Press, 1994.

Theissen, Thomas D. *The Phase I Archeological Research Program for the Knife River Indian Villages National Historic Site.* Lincoln NE: National Park Service, Midwest Archaeological Center, 1993.

Thompson, Edwin N. *Fort Union Trading Post: Fur Trade Empire on the Upper Missouri.* Williston ND: Fort Union Association, 1986.

Utley, Robert M. *Frontier Regulars: The United States Army and the Indian, 1866–1891.* New York: Macmillan, 1973.

———. *Frontiersmen in Blue: The United States Army and the Indian, 1848–1865.* New York: Macmillan, 1967.

Vigil, Ralph H., Frances W. Kaye, and John R. Wunder, eds. *Spain and the Plains: Myths and Realities of Spanish Exploration and Settlement on the Great Plains.* Niwot: University Press of Colorado, 1994.

Willey, Patrick S. *Prehistoric Warfare on the Great Plains: Skeletal Analysis of the Crow Creek Massacre Victims.* New York: Garland, 1990.

Wishart, David J. *Encyclopedia of the Great Plains.* Lincoln: University of Nebraska Press, 2004.

———. *Encyclopedia of the Great Plains Indians.* Lincoln: University of Nebraska Press, 2007.

———. *The Fur Trade of the American West, 1807–1840: A Geographical Synthesis.* Lincoln: University of Nebraska Press, 1979.

———. *Great Plains Indians.* Lincoln: University of Nebraska Press, 2016.

Wood, W. Raymond, ed. *Archaeology on the Great Plains.* Lawrence: University Press of Kansas, 1998.

Wood, W. Raymond, and Thomas D. Thiessen. *Early Fur Trade on the Northern Plains.* Norman: University of Oklahoma Press, 1985.

INDEX

Page numbers in italics indicate illustrations

Fort Astoria, xxxii

Fort Atkinson, 41–42; establishment of, 83–84; site guide for, 149, 163. *See also* Fort Berthold II

Fort Aubrey, site guide for, 149

Fort Augustus, 112; site guide for, 133

Fort Bascom, site guide for, 167

Fort Battleford, site guide for, 141

Fort Bayard, 79

Fort Belknap, 86, 90; site guide for, 154, 183

Fort Bellefontaine, 36

Fort Belmont, site guide for, 149

Fort Bennett, site guide for, 178

Fort Benton (Fort Lewis), 17, 46, 52, 72, 118, 120 21, 123, 125, 153; NWMP and, 122; ranching and, 77; site guide for, 154; steamboats to, 119; trade at, 30, 76–78

Fort Bernard, site guide for, 192

Fort Bertold I, 44; site guide for, 169

Fort Bertold II (Fort Atkinson), site guide for, 169

Fort Bliss, 68, 69, 79; site guide for, 183

Fort Bourbon, 111; building, xxvi

Fort Bridger, 62, 85; refuge at, xxxiii

Fort Brooks, site guide for, 149

Fort Brown, 89–90

Fort Browning, site guide for, 155

Fort Brulé, site guide for, 178

Fort Buford, site guide for, 170

Fort Burgwin, site guide for, 167

Fort Calgary, 124; site guide for, 133

Fort Campbell, 52; site guide for, 155

Fort Carlton, 112, 113; North-West Rebellion and, 126; site guide for, 141

Fort Carondelet, 28–30, 33–34, 36

Fort Carroll, site guide for, 155

Fort Carson, 104, 143; site guide for, 144

Fort Caspar, site guide for, 192

Fort Cass: Crow Nation and, xviii; relocation of, xvi; site guide for, 155

Fort C. F. Smith, 22, 94–95; site guide for, 155

Fort Chadbourne, site guide for, 183

Fort Chardon, site guide for, 156

Fort Childs, 63

Fort Claggett (Camp Cook), site guide for, 156

Fort Clark, 42–44, *44*, 90, 101–2; site guide for, 170, 184; steamboat at, 43. *See also* Fort Osage

Fort Clark Trading Post, 43

Fort Clay, site guide for, 192

Fort Clifton, site guide for, 150

Fort Cobb, site guide for, 174

Fort Coffee, site guide for, 174

Fort Coleman (Fort Colorado), site guide for, 184

Fort Collins, site guide for, 144

Fort Colorado. *See* Fort Coleman

Fort Concho, 68, 70, 79–80, 82, 89; site guide for, 184

Fort Conner. *See* Fort Reno

Fort Conrad, 120; site guide for, 156

IN THE DISCOVER THE GREAT PLAINS SERIES

Great Plains Forts
Jay H. Buckley and Jeffery
D. Nokes

Great Plains Weather
Kenneth F. Dewey

Great Plains Geology
R. F. Diffendal Jr.

Great Plains Politics
Peter J. Longo

Great Plains Bison
Dan O'Brien

Great Plains Birds
Larkin Powell

Great Plains Literature
Linda Ray Pratt

Great Plains Indians
David J. Wishart

Discover the Great Plains, a series from the Center for Great
Plains Studies and the University of Nebraska Press, offers concise
introductions to the natural wonders, diverse cultures, history,
and contemporary life of the Great Plains. To order or obtain
more information on these or other University of Nebraska Press
titles, visit nebraskapress.unl.edu.

Printed in the USA
CPSIA information can be obtained
at www.ICGtesting.com
LVHW012136201023
761447LV00003B/3

9 781496 207715